Robert Sommer

Farmers Markets of America

Let us never forget that the cultivation of the earth is the most important labor of man. When tillage begins other arts follow. The farmers, therefore, are the founders of civilization.

—DANIEL WEBSTER.

Friends are like melons. Shall I tell you why?
To find one good one, you must a hundred try.

—CLAUDE MERMET, Epigram of Friends.

Fruits & Vegies at Their Best · Chart of Seasons · Shopping Hints · Vegie Cookbook

Farmers Markets of America *A Renaissance*

Robert Sommer

Capra Press
Santa Barbara / 1980

Grateful acknowledgements:
Cover photo by Mac McRae.
Special thanks to Virgil Elliott
of Tri-County Produce, Santa Barbara,
and to Patricia Collier of Castle & Cooke
Foods, San Francisco, for Chapter 5.
Also to John and Diane Smith, Bonnie Barr,
Lyn and Nan Cadwell, and Molly Young.

Library of Congress Cataloging in Publication Data
Sommer, Robert.
   Farmers markets of America.
   Bibliography: p.
   1. Farm produce—United States—Marketing.
2. Markets—United States, I. Title.
HD9005.S65   381'.41'0973   79-28507
ISBN 0-88496-150-8

CAPRA PRESS
Post Office Box 2068
Santa Barbara, California 93120

CONTENTS

Foreword

This book connects several facets of my life both in subject matter and approach. It is a mixture of research, experience, opinion, advice, and celebration, not necessarily in that order. I have never believed that social research need be dull or celebration should ignore facts or figures. Whatever wisdom the book contains is a distillation of the experience of markets across the nation.

This cannot be a farmers market guidebook for the whole nation because such a compendium is not feasible. Many states publish seasonal maps and directories showing the location of farmers markets, including the days and hours of operation. These change so often that a national guidebook would be out of date before it was printed. Local people don't need guidebooks because they know where their markets are located. Tourists don't need them because they can always obtain this information locally. Two Japanese writers who visited markets around the world found that "everywhere we went, anyone could direct us to the market place. Once there, we found that without effort or strain we met the ordinary people of each nation." For a nation so diverse, it is comforting to know you can find a sense of continuity in the market place of the people.

I owe a considerable debt to friends who visited and photographed farmers markets in their communities and to my associates in Davis who interviewed customers, growers, market managers, and made the price comparisons. I would like to express special appreciation to Sue Aitkens, Terry Amick, Frank Becker, Harry Caldwell, Robert Dewar, Alan Elms, Hart Guenther, John Herrick, Margaret Hill, Bill Hohn, Yvonne Hunter, Dave Kenny, Ralph Keyes, Walter Kleeman, Heidi Knight, John Newman, Sam Sloan, Barbara Sommer, Ted Sommer, David Stea, Richard Straus, Margot Stumpf, Jason Tyburczy, Jack Williams, and Margaret Wing.

ROBERT SOMMER

'Tis the farmer's care
That makes the field bear.

—THOMAS FULLER, Gnomologia.

Farmers Markets of America

1: THE VIRTUES OF COMMUNITY MARKETS

The farmers market is an old institution being revived to fit new times. It is developing not out of nostalgia but because of what it offers—lower prices to the consumer, higher returns to the producer, fresher produce, an exciting shopping experience, a means to help revitalize downtown areas, and an opportunity for city and country people to come together. That combination of advantages is proving irresistible to communities across the nation where farmers markets are springing up in public parks, empty parking lots, on county fairgrounds, and in courthouse squares. Most are seasonal enterprises, running weekly during the summer months, but a few operate year round selling firewood, Christmas trees, maple syrup, jams and jellies, dried fruit, stored melons, pumpkins, squashes, and apples during the winter months. Each market takes its form from the community and region in which it is held. Markets in southern states offer black-eyed peas, sweet potatoes, and okra. Those in the Southwest sell cactus leaves, chilies, cilantro, homemade salsa, and more. The San Francisco market with its many Asian and East Indian sellers attracts customers who seek sugarcane, bok choy, daikon, and winter melon.

The Massachusetts Department of Food and Agriculture has assisted in the establishment of more than thirty community markets around the state. There are presently eleven Greenmarkets in New York City attracting farmers from as far away as Pennsylvania, New Jersey, and Connecticut. No fewer than five markets are held in Hartford, Connecticut, during the summer months. In the summer of 1978, twenty-six food fairs were operating in Tennessee and Alabama, up from eighteen in 1977, and four in 1976, in which farmers sold directly to the public. West Virginia established seven permanent farmers markets in different cities, and the state provides the staff to run them. The Pennsylvania Department of Agriculture has helped to establish over a dozen tailgate markets for farmers selling directly to the public. The Honolulu city government sponsors twenty People's Open Markets on city-owned land selling fruits, vegetables, baked goods, meat and fish farmed by Filipino, Samoan, Vietnamese, and other ethnic groups. The Province of Alberta, Canada, operates two programs to assist farmers markets. The first provides grants to gardeners and fresh vegetable producers who grow crops to be sold directly to the public. To be eligible for a grant, a gardener must work at least two acres of land. The Alberta Market Place Program provides grants through the Provincial Department of Agriculture to organizations and individuals who sponsor farmers markets.

Madison, WISCONSIN

There are numerous reasons behind this renewed interest in direct farm sales. Our research at markets in fifteen California cities showed that farmers market prices were 34% lower than those at supermarkets. When one realizes that fruit and vegetables displayed on supermarket counters may have been transported hundreds or thousands of miles and loaded and unloaded five times before they reach the counter, significant price savings in direct sales are understandable. One economist estimated that 80% of the retail cost of supermarket produce goes to wholesalers, jobbers, packers, and transporters, not to mention the waxers, colorists, and gassers who treat produce from factory farms to make it look palatable.

With increasing energy costs, transportation charges to farmers are rising, making local crops more competitive with those shipped in from distant regions. Local producers and local markets are social buffers in times of crisis. A century ago, Connecticut produced 80% of its own food supplies. Today 85% of Connecticut food is imported from outside the state and often from outside the nation. The same is true in New Hampshire whose citizens would be in serious trouble in the event of a transportation tie-up in some part of the nation or an oil shortage that reduced truck shipments into the state.

The best protection against control of the American food industry by an international cartel is a healthy, decentralized system of small farms and local markets. If the experience of international cartels in oil, coffee, or uranium is any guide, the American subsidiaries of multinational corporations are more likely to work with cartels than to oppose them. Local producers selling to consumers at local markets would aid the nation in times of crisis and protect against cartels that would control distribution as well as production.

Local markets are a means of preserving regional specialty crops and varieties unsuitable for the factory farm. Growers at a farmers market don't carry a single variety of iceberg lettuce whose primary attribute is its ability to withstand thousands of miles of transport and still look attractive. Instead community markets carry red lettuce, bib lettuce, butter lettuce, endive, collard and dandelion greens. They also offer Silver Queen corn, Country Gentleman corn, stumpy and lumpy corn, and multi-hued Indian corn for table decorations. The wholesale marketing system tends toward uniformity and standardization. There are

Springfield, ILLINOIS

many farmers who want to raise a certain variety of fruit because it grows well in their orchards and they have always raised it as their parents and grandparents had before them, but packing houses won't buy it and shippers won't transport it. The only outlet for such produce is direct sale to the public.

The term farmers market has been badly abused by mass marketers. Confusion in the public mind about the nature of a farmers market is partly a result of commercial institutions deliberately trying to capitalize upon its good image. There is a large supermarket chain in California that calls itself Farmers Markets that is indistinguishable from any other chain. When First National Stores observed the popularity of community markets in Massachusetts, they began placing cases of fruits and vegetables on their parking lots and shaded them with beach umbrellas. A century ago, a farmers market had a clear meaning. I am hopeful this will happen again.

American open air markets have a distinctive visual geometry based on the scale and requirements of the pickup truck. In some communities they are called tailgate sales or curb days. Trucks line up side-by-

Stockton, CALIFORNIA

side facing outward, tailgates opened to the sidewalk revealing a cornucopia of delicious fresh fruits and vegetables. The Columbus Park market in Kenosha, Wisconsin, consists of a single row of fifty pickup trucks backed to the sidewalk. Our local market in Davis follows the same geometry although on a smaller scale. This arrangement allows selling directly from the tailgate without the need for unloading except for display purposes. Empty crates and baskets are piled alongside the cab and later in the front of the storage bed as the produce is sold off. The area around the cab is the seller's turf, the sidewalk belongs to customers, and the space at the tailgate is the meeting ground between buyer and seller.

Descriptions of markets in other nations always include pungent and exciting odors—raw fish, spicy meat dishes cooking in large pots, earthy smells of fresh vegetables, the fetid odor of over-ripe fruit, and the heat of crowds engaged in basic human activities. Americans are a non-olfactory people and our community markets express this. Outdoor markets here are bereft of strong odors and the excitement and stimulation are visual, social, and economic rather than olfactory. The situation is different in enclosed public buildings such as the Atlanta Municipal Market whose atmosphere is dominated by the sale of pig products or Seattle's Pike Place Market where customers throng to buy fresh fish.

American markets are quieter and more subdued than their counterparts in other lands. One reason is that the sellers are farmers rather than professional hawkers and mongers. While farmers are friendly and helpful, they tend to be taciturn people. Instead of loud cries extolling the virtues of their produce they are more apt to rely on the quiet offer of a free sample or free taste.

2: THE VEGIE REVOLUTION:

With Some Historical Perspective

Vegetables used to be what you ate because they were good for you. A meal wasn't complete without a green vegetable, but there was nothing special about *fresh* vegetables. Weren't the frozen peas supposed to be flash frozen immediately after picking and the corn kernels canned at the peak of flavor? At least this is what Madison Avenue told us.

The per capita consumption of fresh fruits and vegetables has dropped by almost half since 1920. No wonder, since many young people don't know what really fresh produce tastes like. They have been raised on foods in cans and freezer packages. Once a grower friend of mine gave samples of his apricots to ten people who passed by his stall. Three had never tasted a fresh apricot before. Previously, the same farmer had found some of his roadside-stand customers unwilling to taste fruit from a tree. These deprived people regarded apricots on the tree as inedible, believing they had to be cooked or frozen or mashed or mixed with sugar before they could be eaten. Television advertising is partly responsible for this alienation from fresh produce. When is the last time you saw a commercial for whole tomatoes or whole apples? Barbecue-flavored ketchup or frozen apple pie are advertised but not fresh tomatoes and

fresh apples. Sunkist doesn't advertise oranges as much as it advertises orange juice. Products which are sold fresh, such as celery and lettuce, rarely appear on the TV screen, and there are obviously many more advertisements for dressings than for the other ingredients of a salad. Many supermarket managers believe that young Americans don't even know how to cook fresh vegetables. After all there are no instructions on a head of cauliflower or cabbage.

I had not appreciated the taste of fresh vegetables until several years ago when my curiosity led me to our city park in Davis, California, to investigate the Saturday farmers market. I found the low prices very attractive, but it is the quality of the produce that has kept me returning week after week. Like many other customers, my appreciation of the flavor of fresh vegetables came *after* rather than before I started buying directly from growers.

Seattle, WASHINGTON

18

What A Farmers Market Is

Farmers markets are called by many names—Community Farm Markets in Illinois, Food Fairs in Alabama and Louisiana, Court Day in Wisconsin, where they follow the route of the circuit court through the county, Curb Markets and Trade Days in the Northeast, and Certified Farmers Markets in California. The true farmers market, as the term is used here, is a place where those who grow food sell it directly to consumers. Ambiguity arises when we attempt to go further than this limited definition. What if some farmers sell partly their own crops and partly those of neighbors? How about farmers who sell some of their own crops as well as non-seasonal items that are purchased from wholesale produce terminals? What if some farmers sell their own produce alongside retail stands which purchase through the commercial market? What about the sale of baked goods, maple syrup and sorghum, and arts and crafts? In the state of Washington, several Saturday Markets sell 80% crafts and 20% produce. Seattle's bustling Pike Place Market has farmers selling their own crops at low tables paying reduced stall rates, while produce retailers sell at high tables at higher rates.

History

The first American farmers markets were copies of their European cousins. Farmers came into town in horse-drawn wagons to sell their crops to city dwellers. Most of the selling initially took place on open lots along a major thoroughfare which became Market Street. Soon closed sheds protected temporary stalls, but these, in turn, gave

way to large buildings on land donated to the farmers by the city or by a wealthy citizen. In Europe it is still usual to find communities sponsoring market days, and these are usually scheduled so that farmers can make a weekly circuit of three or four towns in a given region. Public markets are also commonplace in developing nations where direct sales still play a major role in the economy.

The first market on record in the English colonies was established in 1634 in Boston by order of Governor John Winthrop, and a wooden building was constructed for the market in 1658. Faneuil Hall market building was completed in 1742 and enlarged several times after that. Philadelphia had the distinction of having the best planned and regulated markets in the colonies. William Penn's plans for the city included a market along the main thoroughfare, High Street, later renamed Market Street. According to the original proclamation in 1693, the market was opened twice weekly by the ringing of a bell and no one was permitted to buy or sell on the way to the market.

Syracuse, NEW YORK

18th c. marketplace
in "Aldstadt" (old part of town)

Colonial markets guaranteed equal access to all producers. This was insured by a "king's peace" and later by a "market peace" enforced by a market master or special market court. Pillories were constructed for those who violated its laws and were used for offenses such as *forestalling* which meant attempting to privately purchase goods before they reached the market; *engrossing,* or attempting to create a monopoly in order to limit supply and control prices; and *regrating* which was buying "dead victuals" at a market for the purpose of reselling them at the same market. The prohibition against regrating was largely a sanitary measure intended to minimize the amount of rehandling of perishable foods.

As an inducement to their formation, markets were protected in various other ways. Some cities prohibited the sale of competitive products during the hours that the public market was open, while others prohibited stores from being established within a quarter mile of any public market or prohibited pushcart vendors from selling competitive products on the streets during market hours.

The Royal Charter of Incorporation for the Common Market in St. John, New Brunswick, was awarded in 1785. This is believed to be the oldest formal grant for such a purpose in Canada. The present buildings were constructed in 1876 and are still in use as a public market. The Richmond, Virginia, farmers market has been in continuous operation for over 180 years. It is located in downtown Richmond, and the area is maintained by the city which issues daily selling permits to producers. Wisconsin's first community market began in Racine in 1834, and Watertown, Wisconsin, has been holding Fair Days on the second Tuesday of each month continuously for the past 130 years. Most early markets permitted livestock trading along with the sale of produce.

The public market reached its peak during the nineteenth century and then declined swiftly. The growth of cities brought new health and sanitation regulations and architectural codes that many of the large older structures could not meet without enormous capital outlays. It often seemed more economical to tear down a building than to renovate it. Improved transportation and the development of refrigeration techniques made it possible to ship crops long distances. Suburban development began to chew up much of the land around the city previously cultivated by gardeners and farmers. The creation of food chain stores was a heavy blow to small farmers who had sold at the public market. A regional warehouse was not interested in a load of near-ripe melons or cherries. They turned instead to factory farms at distant locations capable of delivering fruits and vegetables at specific times that could travel long distances and maintain their appearance through numerous loadings and unloadings. Neighborhoods that had played such an important role in maintaining local markets lost their economic power to the central business district.

Researchers at land grant colleges encouraged these trends by developing varieties of crops for volume production that would withstand the long delay between harvest and sale, as well as special treatments to maintain the appearance of food in transit and storage. Researchers focused on issues of major concern to agribusiness and did little for the small producer who could not afford expensive machinery or keep abreast of all the new chemical processes for increasing yield, eliminating blemishes, and artifically ripening produce. To the argument that the small producer

Newark, NEW JERSEY

was on the way out anyway, one can only emphasize that agribusiness-oriented research contributed to the trend.

However, the public market probably would not have been undermined without changes that were occurring in consumer attitudes. Mass advertising by food chains altered buying and eating habits. Convenience became the byword in mass retailing. A supermarket contained, under one roof, everything the average household needed, readily available for quick inspection, purchase, and checkout. Customers turned away from the local grocers who had been the mainstays of support for small farmers and instead patronized supermarkets supplied by factory farms.

The public market declined rapidly throughout the nation. Some of the best loved buildings were torn down and the land sold to developers. The district commission in Washington, D.C. rented the Georgetown Farmers Market to an automotive parts company, even though the property had been deeded to the city in 1802 with the provision that it remain a public market "forever." Other buildings were preserved at the cost of conversion into boutiques and specialty shops with rents far beyond the means of small farmers. What happened in Indianapolis is illustrative of this pattern.

When Alexander Ralston drew his plot for the town of Indianapolis in 1821, the southern half of Square 43 was reserved for a public market. This is the present site of the Indianapolis City Market. The original building about which little is known was replaced by the present structure in 1886. Business boomed, and in 1892 the market master recommended that the haymarket be removed and the space used for additional vegetable stalls. At the turn of the century, the decline began. Public health officials required extensive improvements

in health and sanitation facilities and the costs of running the market began to increase. Corruption, price fixing, and poor

management also occurred. Plans were drawn to demolish the building and replace it with an office complex. Lawsuits were instituted on both sides which reached all the way to the US Supreme Court in 1968. At that point, a new mayor and new market master began a major renovation program whose objective it was to "get the market into the black." Their efforts succeeded. The venture became self-supporting in 1969 and has remained economically healthy since then. However, the character of the present complex is very different from that of its predecessors. It is no longer a place where farmers come to sell their foodstuffs. Of the present sixty stalls, half sell jewelry, gifts, clothing, greeting cards, and sundries. The remaining stands consist of five each selling general groceries, produce, and meat, two fish stands, two cheese stands—all of which secure most of their produce from wholesale channels—three flower and plant stores, and four ice cream stands. The market building has been saved and is now a registered architectural landmark, but it has lost its original purpose.

The situation was somewhat different in small towns where at least some farm sales had been in continuous operation for over a century, but the urban consumer in the early twentieth century had lost the opportunity to buy food directly from small producers.

During the turbulent 1960s one of the targets of disenchanted consumers was the domination of agriculture as well as many other segments of the economy by multinational corporations. Legislators began seeking ways to help improve the situation of small family farmers. Consumer groups and some agricultural economists were proving that large scale agriculture did not necessarily benefit the consumer. The agricultural policies of the Consumer Federation of America are based "on the conviction that what is good for the family farmer is good for consumers . . .and the consumer's right to quality food at reasonable prices is threatened as family farmers are driven out of business."

Urban consumers were particularly vulnerable to increases in food prices since they lacked land on which to grow their own vegetables. Politicians found that criticism of the food price-spread had considerable appeal to the voters who could not understand why farmers were receiving lower prices for food that cost more at the checkout stand.

The nation was also becoming aware of the dangers of pesticides. DDT was banned and serious questions were raised about many of the other sprays. Consumer groups lobbied for labeling of additives and regulations regarding acceptable levels of pesticides. Customers began to look for unsprayed produce that was unavailable in the supermarket.

Americans responded to these challenges in many ways. Community gardens were created in vacant lots to supply fresh produce to neighborhood residents. The US Department of Agriculture established special programs to assist small producers. The farmers market resurgence is another response to the consolidation of economic power in the food industry. Like any other single measure, it cannot solve all the problems that have developed. On the other hand, the establishment of local markets is clearly a progressive step that can accomplish as much by example as by its tangible benefits to small growers and consumers.

While there is no likelihood that farmers markets can replace the wholesale distribution system, they will remain an alternative and incremental outlet for both producer and consumer. The importance of such alternatives is that they provide comparison points for the dominant system. This role is far more significant for society than the actual dollar volume of all direct marketing operations. Alternative systems provide consumers and policy makers with a standard by which the commercial system can be judged. Farmers markets are not a fad, unless you consider families trying to save money and eat better or farmers trying to survive as a fad.

Davis, CALIFORNIA

Springfield, ILLINOIS

FINDING A FARMERS MARKET

Farmers markets go by different names in different parts of the country. Reliable information can be obtained from the local chamber of commerce, the county extension agent, or a state department of agriculture. It will be necessary for you to explain that you are looking for a place where small farmers sell fruits and vegetables to the public. Watch out that you are not directed to a wholesale operation. While there are a few combined wholesale-retail outlets such as the Shelby County Farmers Market near Memphis, most wholesale outlets do not sell directly to the public. Many state departments of agriculture publish yearly directories of markets showing location, selling hours, days, and main products available. This information is likely to be accurate only for a single season.

When you get to a market, you should establish that the seller has actually grown the produce. Roadside stands buy much of their produce on the wholesale market. This is also true of many people selling from the backs of trucks at flea markets or alongside the highway. When a farmers market is listed by a state department of agriculture, there is a good likelihood that the seller is actually the grower. The only way to learn this in a specific case is to ask directly.

Davis, CALIFORNIA

Kenosha, WISCONSIN

3: BENEFITS FOR THE SMALL GROWERS

The farmer's share of the consumer dollar has decreased significantly. Fifty years ago the farmer received anywhere from 50–80¢ of every dollar spent on fresh fruits and vegetables. Today that figure is less than 30¢ and still dropping. Farmers perceive themselves increasingly at the mercy of a marketing system dominated by the chains which establish prices and set quality standards appropriate for factory farms. Those farmers who sell directly to the public find that they can receive higher returns and still give the consumer a bargain. A study in the state of Washington showed that marketing costs of several vegetables were lowest for U-pick, next lowest in selling to a processor or on the wholesale market, and highest for a farmer-run roadside stand or selling at a farmers market. Roadside stand costs were increased by the high cost of labor and selling at the farmers market by the high costs of transportation. However, costs are only one side of the ledger. As Table 1 shows, the returns in selling strawberries directly to the public are sometimes much higher than for selling on the wholesale market. Taking into account the increased expenses for time and travel, the profit margin at the farmers market is almost three times better than at the wholesale market.

Table 1. Marketing Costs and Returns from Washington State Strawberries*

Marketing Method	Marketing Cost (per pound)	Price Received (per pound)	Difference
Processor	0.130	0.270	0.140
Wholesale	0.220	0.375	0.155
U-pick	0.050	0.300	0.250
Roadside Stand	0.260	0.450	0.190
Farmers Market	0.240	0.670	0.430

*Adapted from C.J. Moulton, King County Agricultural Marketing Study, October, 1977.

Without the extra money from a roadside stand, pick-your-own orchard, or a farmers market, many small growers would be forced off the land. Ervin Geils has a moderate sized farm in Des Plaines, Illinois, and sells at five farmers markets in the area. When he began farming in 1942, he delivered his truckloads to commission houses in Chicago and to local canneries and also sold wholesale to roadside stands, produce markets, and grocery stores. By the late 1950s, high commissions, high transportation costs, and rigid container specifications reduced profits on sales to canneries and commission houses. Urban growth and rising land values had forced the closure of many of the roadside stands in the area. To compensate for these losses in his wholesale business, Geils opened a fruit stand on his own farm which became the major outlet for his crops. Subsequently he opened satellite stands at rented locations in nearby communities. These rental operations were costly and there was no guarantee of yearly renewal.

When the opportunity arose to participate in the Evanston, Illinois, Farmers Market, Geils took it. The initial cost of $75 for a seasonal stall rental was the only investment at risk. The market was an immediate and overwhelming success. Geils found the advantages so great that he subsequently rented stall locations at other farmers markets in the vicinity. One nice feature is ready, immediate cash—no bad checks, credit, or delays in collecting money from wholesale houses. Geils sets his own prices based on quality, competition, and demand. He doesn't have to pay handling charges or commissions, except for modest stall rentals. Container costs are minimal since many customers bring their own shopping bags. In 1979 the Geils family planted 200 acres of vegetables, including several varieties of each with different ripening periods. Sixteen varieties of sweet corn were intended to extend the selling season and minimize the damage that could be done by pests, such as the southern leaf blight which had damaged three corn varieties in the past.

Farmers selling at the Detroit Eastern Farmers Market consider this outlet preferable to wholesale warehouses because it is less demanding (you can show up three days one week and not at all the next week) and more convenient since it provides an opportunity to sell all the crops at a single location with a minimum of sorting, labeling, and grading. It is more dependable than selling to chain stores which can cancel orders or "kick off" produce that does not meet their standards, and is also more profitable and more enjoyable. Dealing with various levels of jobbers and wholesalers, the individual farmer has very little control over critical issues such as price, delivery date, or packing. Selling directly to the public, the farmer can control these factors.

A survey of small farmers, most of whom engaged in direct marketing, found that they were farmers because; 1) they appreciate being their own boss; 2) they enjoy the physical work; 3) a farm is a good place to raise a family; 4) they like the people in the farm community; 5) they need the income derived from farming; and 6) they believe the equity being built in the land will pay off when they retire. It seems noteworthy that feelings of independence and enjoyment of their way of life are a small farmer's primary motivations.

San Francisco, CALIFORNIA

Young Farmers, Old Farmers

Many young sellers are the children and grandchildren of farmers. Denny Geils whom I met selling at the Evanston, Illinois, market is the son of Ervin Geils mentioned earlier, and is a fifth generation farmer. However, some young sellers are not from farm families. Although many cannot afford to own land and farm full-time, they have, nevertheless, chosen a rural life. Usually someone in the household has an outside job. They may start by leasing several acres or sharecropping, several couples buying land together, or growing food in community gardens. Children of the ecology movement, they are interested in the environment and getting close to nature. Some try to farm organically, but most use pesticides in small amounts when needed. In my area, the average plot of land being farmed by these young farmers is less than ten acres, and some work intensively on plots of two acres and less. 50-100 varieties of fruits or vegetables which ripen throughout the entire growing season may be planted, but never more of a single crop than can be sold locally. Young farmers tend to give their operations funky names like Good Humus, Mr. Cleanjeans, Chicken Rick, and The Good Earth Cooperative. Their hands—strong, calloused, dirt-encrusted—set them apart from other young people of their generation. Selling at a farmers market means getting up at 3:00 A.M. to pick, load, and arrive at 7:00. After the main rush of customers has passed, sellers take turns minding each other's trucks, so that one of them can catch up on sleep.

At some of the markets I visited, such as the cooperatively-owned sales building in South Bend, Indiana, the typical seller was in his or her sixties. A strong bond exists between the old timers and the youngsters selling at the markets, much like the attachment between grandparents and grandchildren. The old farmers offer the wisdom of their experience, and at any market you can find middle-aged customers scouting things out, earnestly seeking information about the economics of part-time farming. One couple, a former aerospace engineer and a former librarian, has been asked so often about the economics of their honey operation that they can recite the figures by heart. Their 60-hive apiary is many people's retirement dream. Contact with nature and the production of something useful appeals to many people today.

Kenosha, WISCONSIN

Davis, CALIFORNIA

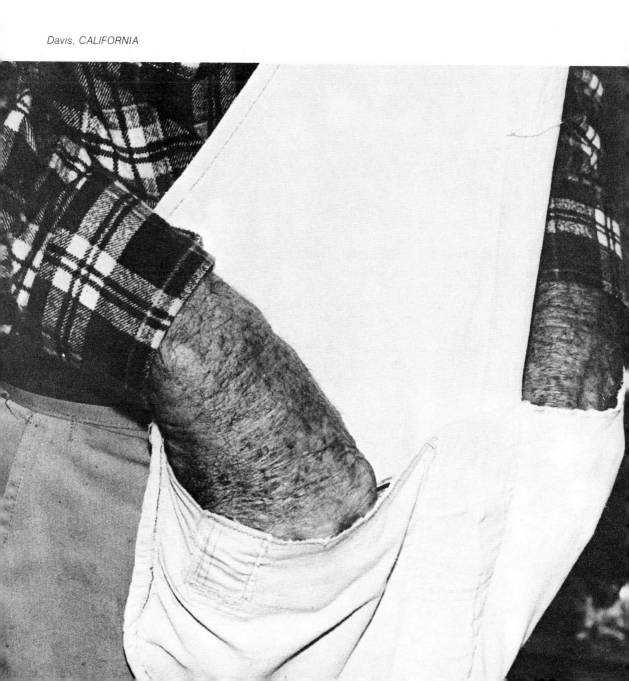

Many older sellers enjoy being part of a trading economy. Having a garden is not sufficient challenge; they relish the bargaining. "Not many people are bargaining," complained the elderly apple seller. He enjoyed the give-and-take of a hard bargain and wondered aloud whether he should put up a sign, "Make me an offer." At a deep level, he worried that his own trading skills, so finely honed over several decades of active wheeling and dealing, would fall into disuse. It wasn't that he was complaining about the prices that he received. Indeed it was the opposite lament—people were willing to pay the asked price without question. My friend rarely posted his prices because he wanted customers to ask. Many city people are not used to this practice. Accustomed to the anonymity and impersonality of the supermarket, they expect a sign showing the name and price of each item.

My friend attempted to teach customers how to bargain: how to maintain the right posture and expression, how to question the quality of the merchandise. "Anytime you see a slight discoloration, you can ask for a lower price. If the items are too small, too big, misshapen, last in the bin, picked over, or not sorted—you can always find some reason to push prices down." My friend is disturbed that so many customers don't even try to get the best value for their money. Occasionally he parries a question about price with another, "What do you think they're worth?" or "What are you willing to pay?" The inexperienced shopper mumbles something and walks away with an uncomfortable look on his face. I don't want to leave the impression that all customers are greenhorns who pay whatever is asked without question. Some enjoy driving a hard bargain as much as my friend does and will deliberately arrive at the market late in the day to bid a low price on whatever remains.

Ithaca, NEW YORK

Prices are set by growers based on what is charged at the grocery store and what others are receiving. A few older sellers who have been farming commercially for decades read daily wholesale price reports and adjust their own prices accordingly. When a farmer is charging too much, customers will let him or her know quickly. It is equally embarrassing for a farmer to realize

Greenmarket 59th St. New York City, NEW YORK

Syracuse, NEW YORK

that his or her prices are too low. I overheard one grower remark to another, "If I'd known you were getting 10¢ more for peaches, I'd have asked that much too." She was indignant that she had not been able to realize the best price.

Community markets also create sales opportunities for backyard gardeners who have filled their tables, freezers, and neighbors' needs, and still have produce left over. Home gardeners are not perceived as competitors by small farmers providing they sell at the prevailing prices. The problem in most farmers markets is not too many but too few growers competing with one another. Home gardeners are among the most avid customers for items they do not grow themselves. Once you're hooked on really fresh vegetables, it's hard to go back to those from the supermarket.

There is strong opposition to farmers from other regions who attempt to dump surplus commodities at low prices. Farmers will receive the best price for something early in the season when it is in scarce supply. This bonus from early crops will be lost if sellers from regions with earlier harvest dates sell large quantities which are at their seasonal peak. Some markets try to prevent dumping by restricting sellers to those residing in the county or from a fifty-mile radius. However, market organizers also recognize the value of farmers from other regions who can provide some variety to customers. Within a single county where everybody raises pears or plums, the local market will be glutted. The best opportunity for local growers with an oversupply is to travel to nearby counties where items are in short supply. The one practice that all markets seek to avoid is dumping of seconds from the wholesale market. If permitted, this practice will quickly erode the market's reputation for quality produce.

4: CONSUMER BENEFITS

The three top reasons for the popularity of farmers markets are food quality, price savings, and social atmosphere. First and foremost, the customers care about the taste of what they eat and value flavor and freshness over convenience. Price is the second reason why people buy directly from farmers. Systematic comparisons of item-by-item prices charged at supermarkets and certified farmers markets in fifteen California cities have shown that the farmers market prices are substantially lower. The average per unit price for produce items in supermarkets was $0.70 compared to $0.46 at these farmers markets.

This 34% overall price saving is a conservative figure. It does not include the baker's dozens given at farmers markets, the rounding which is always in the customer's favor (four and a half pounds of apples charged as four pounds, 53¢ rounded off to 50¢), the discounts given for quantity purchases (six melons for the price of five), or the deep discounts traditional at the end of the market day won by a customer driving a hard bargain.

Figure 2 shows that the farmers market price was lower than the supermarket price 91% of the time, the supermarket price was lower 8% of the time, and the prices at the two outlets were equal 1% of the time.

Researchers in other regions have also documented price savings. Supermarket prices in Hartford, Conn., averaged from 29-46% higher than the average price of those same items at farmers markets. Studies in four Southeastern states (North Carolina, West Virginia, Virginia, and Tennessee) showed that farmers market prices averaged 28% lower than prices for the same items at the supermarket. A study of food fairs held at twenty-two towns and cities in Tennessee and Alabama during the summer of 1977, showed a 50% average saving on produce under retail cost. A food price survey in Seattle showed an average price saving at the Pike Place Market of 8% compared to prices at five supermarkets.

American markets provide a happy exception to the two-pricing system found in markets in other nations where tourists are charged more than locals for the same items. Nothing like this is found at community markets in the United States where any customer, tourist or local, can bring prices down through bargaining.

A relevant issue is whether the quality of the produce is equivalent at farmers markets and supermarkets. If farmers market customers are paying less money for lower grade produce, then the price savings aren't very meaningful except to bargain hunters. However, there is no question that farmers market produce is fresher and more flavorful. Much of it has been picked earlier on the day it is sold. There is nothing comparable in national supermarkets, where the produce has been picked a week

Figure 1

Supermarket average unit price

70¢

Farmers market average unit price

46¢

Savings to consumers → 34% 24¢

Figure 2

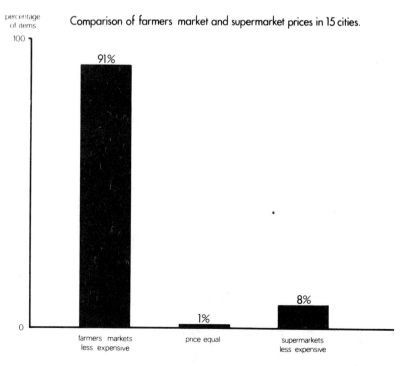

percentage
of items

Comparison of farmers market and supermarket prices in 15 cities.

100

91%

1%

8%

0

farmers markets
less expensive

price equal

supermarkets
less expensive

earlier, hauled around the country, and loaded and unloaded several times.

The issue of flavor is complex, but existing evidence favors farmers market produce. Sugars in corn turn quickly to starch once the ear is picked. Therefore, because farmers market corn is fresher, it is also sweeter. The riper a tomato when it is picked, the more sugars it will have. Most farmers market tomatoes are vine-ripened while many in the supermarket have been picked green and ripened artificially using ethylene gas. Research has shown that green-picked tomatoes have less sugars and are less sweet and palatable than tomatoes picked ripe. We attempted some systematic laboratory studies of customer taste preferences for farmers market and supermarket produce. Early results showed that farmers market bell peppers were preferred over supermarket bell peppers and the results from tomatoes were equivocal. Subsequent results have shown two-to-one preference of farmers market over supermarket tomatoes in closely supervised laboratory-type flavor comparisons.

Eating seasonally and adjusting one's diet to the rhythm of the local growing seasons is easier than it sounds. When local asparagus is in season, it is a great value at 25¢ a pound and it is fragrant, crisp, and sweet to the palate. For about a month, we may have asparagus two or three times a week. This also happens during the brief boysenberry season when the juicy tart berries are added to the morning's cereal, using as topping over ice cream, cooked for pies and cobblers, and eaten fresh as a snack. They are a splendid buy at 30¢ a basket. During the corn season, sweet fresh corn is on our table several times a week.

Since I have been shopping at farmers markets, my seventeen-year old daughter has become a vegetable junkie. Her typical lunch consists of steamed vegetables covered with grated cheese. This is quite a change from the convenience foods of junior high days when the evening's entertainment was a visit to Jack-in-the-Box with her friends. Her improved eating habits alone are almost sufficient incentive to keep me going back to community markets.

I don't mean to imply that we never buy anything out of season or from distant regions. However, we do restrict our purchase of fresh tomatoes from late May (the early ones) to November when the last dregs from the fields are sold at reduced prices. Some farmers market customers buy produce for canning, freezing or drying, but this is more the exception than the rule. Our surveys disclosed that while 40% of the

customers occasionally buy food for home processing, they primarily buy fruits and vegetables for table use. Those who are serious home processors are likely to patronize a U-pick operation where prices are even lower.

What little evidence exists on the issue of appearance runs in the other direction. In general, produce in the supermarket has fewer blemishes and fits a standard "ideal shape." Many varieties sold at a farmers market look odd or funny, lumpy or bumpy, off-color and off-size. There is no such thing as an apple that´is too small or too large at a farmers market, nor do growers worry excessively about selling produce that is thin-skinned, bruised or discolored, for the customer accepts these in the interests of improved flavor. Many small growers try to farm organically. This means that some corn ears may have worms in them.

Regular customers know this, and remove the tops before cooking. In fact, when a farmer advertising "organic produce" has corn without any worms at all, customers will become suspicious.

Greenmarket 59th St. New York City, NEW YORK

Specialty items not found on supermarket shelves are often available at farmers markets. On a visit to the Santa Cruz, California, Community Market, there were five kinds of apples for sale, Philippine beans, flats of large speckled turkey eggs sought eagerly not only for their table use but by local artists who paint them. There were cloves of elephant garlic, larger than any I had ever seen. One of the star attractions at the Champaign, Illinois, Community Market is the catfish farmer who has ponds on his land for commercial sales. Although the sale of prepared meat and poultry products is forbidden at our market in Davis, California, several farmers offer live chickens, rabbits, goats, and sheep. The sheep seller is willing to butcher his animals and sell them by the quarter or half, but this activity is done on his farm.

Many community markets have a formal mechanism for exchanging recipes: special sections in monthly news letters, flyers prepared by home economists or nutritionists, or collections of recipes supplied by customers and growers. Almost every market has an information table where you can find free circulars describing food that is available and ways to prepare it to retain the nutrients. A farmer will not be able to sell new varieties of produce unless potential customers are told how to use them. However, I recently met a grower who was selling squash blossoms—because he saw another selling them—even though he did not know exactly what to do with them. I was able to explain that squash blossoms (the infertile male flowers) could be stuffed with cheese, chicken, or ground beef and used as a main course or could be lightly cooked in butter or oil and used as a vegetable. A Hispanic farmer who sells cactus leaves cut into small pieces always cautions his Anglo customers not to cook them too long lest they become slimy. Personally, I prefer them uncooked in salads.

Melon Madness is held in early September at our farmers market. There is a watermelon-eating contest for youngsters as well as usual prizes for outstanding melons. There is an award for the largest and smallest melon and for the oddest looking one. Accustomed to the three standard varieties available in the supermarket (cantaloupe, honeydew, and watermelon) I never realized how many melons are grown locally. There are crenshaw, white crenshaw, honeydew, muskmelon, casaba, klondike watermelon, crane, harboozee, honeyloupe, ambrosia, Ha-Oken, and sugar baby watermelon. I spoke to a grower selling Ha-Okens which are not very exciting in exterior appearance. When she first introduced the Ha-Oken, she had to give away free samples because it looked so ugly on the outside and the skin had a bad odor. The insides, however, are delicious, like a super-sweet honeydew. The Ha-Oken was developed in Israel and I learned there are three varieties—the regular Ha-Oken, the Hemet-Oken, and the Big Oken. Her melons had won several prizes at the county fair and she prominently displayed the ribbons on her truckbed along with the certificate identifying her as a certified farmers market producer.

At the Valparaiso, Indiana, market, held on the courthouse square on Tuesdays and Thursdays, I talked to a farmer selling four kinds of potatoes each carrying an identifying sign: Kennebec—good for baking; Katahdin—the old time favorite; Red La Soda—a good boiler; and the Superior Potato—good for every use. At another market, I talked to a man selling Chippewas which he claimed would not turn black. In the bean category there were limas in the shell, wax beans, Kentucky Wonders, and horticultural beans—which the seller explained is their technical name, although most people call them cranberry, October, or shellout beans. I lost count of all the varieties of apples being sold at a market in Wisconsin. Besides the usual McIntosh, Red Delicious, and Golden Delicious, there were Wisconsin Snows, Wolf River, Greening, Milton, Spartan, Winter Banana, Summer Champion, McMahon, Jon Grimes, Jonathan, Wealthy, Courtland, and Paula apples. I was told that if I had come several months earlier, I would have also found the Viking, the Yellow Transparent, the Lodi, and the Beacon. The US Department of Agriculture lists some 7,000 varieties of apples, but only eight varieties account for three-quarters of all commercial production. Fortunately it is still possible to buy some of the unusual varieties from farmers.

In another conversation, I learned about drying grapes—not only the Thompson variety, but the black monukka which is even sweeter. I was reassured that the white powdery substance on some of our drying grapes was nothing to be afraid of; it was only a yeast related to the sugars and would be useful if we wanted to make wine. I found out how to deal with click beetles and root worms and how to cut back chrysanthemums and dahlias to keep them from becoming rangy.

Besides price savings and improved freshness, customers are attracted by the atmosphere and social encounters, by real farmers selling fruits and vegetables they have raised themselves to customers who care about what they eat, by the farmers' children sitting on trucks and helping to sort, bag, weigh, and make change, and by the comparing and bargaining of an ordinary market day. It is a quintessential democratic institution. People of all ages, races, and social classes rub shoulders and transact business hand-to-hand. The owner of a 500 acre orchard sells alongside a truck gardener who intensively cultivates the tiny plot outside her home. A teenage boy buys apples from a makeshift stand operated by a seventy-year-old apple grower. A senior citizen buys apples from a teenager perched on the top of his parent's pickup truck. College professors and laborers vie with each other over the largest, firm-fleshed bell peppers, the most solid lettuce heads.

Customers find that it is fun to shop at a farmers market. It's a great way to start a Saturday. It's a place to meet friends and neighbors, to talk food and politics, to exchange recipes and gardening practices. Regular customers know one another and are known by name by the sellers. Many always buy their eggs from the same supplier because the shells are brown and always break clean. Each corn seller has a dedicated cadre of buyers. Customers argue with one another over who has the best tomatoes and the sweetest melons.

Children enjoy community markets because they are dynamic places with a myriad of sounds, smells, and tastes. Most growers give children free samples, cut in a grand manner with a huge knife. Senior citizens enjoy the social atmosphere, the give-and-take between sellers and buyers, the per-

sonal service, and the nostalgia of an old-time institution adapted to a new age. At the West Oakland, California, market I met a seventy-eight-year-old woman leaning heavily on her wheelchair, one leg slightly shorter than the other. She bought one or two pieces of fruit from each of several growers, placing them in an orange bucket hanging from one of the wheelchair handles. A friend from her senior citizen hotel wheels her ten blocks to the market every Saturday morning. The trip takes almost an hour. She explains that she comes to the market to "see her friends." Further inquiry reveals that the friends are the farmers. "They know me, I am a regular. I have been here since the market opened." She spends every Saturday morning looking, buying, and visiting. She loves the atmosphere and seeing all the new varieties of fruit.

The early birds among the shoppers are usually goal directed. They walk briskly and are purposeful. Later shoppers are strollers who enjoy the intangibles of the market more fully. Politicians love farmers markets because they are great places to see and be seen. It is common to find activist organizations collecting signatures, handing out leaflets, and engaging passersby in dialogue while selling baked goods to raise money for a campaign. Community markets encourage grassroots democracy. At a farmers

Woodland, CALIFORNIA

market, people are polite and responsive, even if they don't want to contribute, because the market is a friendly place where neighbors meet and talk with one another.

We made a systematic comparison of the social life at nine farmers markets and twenty-six national chain supermarkets in the same cities. We recorded the social encounters that took place in each setting for a total of 171 customers. Encounters were classified into one of three categories: (1) perfunctory (brief, impersonal, and not requiring a reply, like "Excuse me," or "Have a good day."), (2) informational ("How much are these peaches?") and (3) social encounters. There were about the same number of perfunctory interactions in both settings. However, there were three times as many informational encounters at the farmers markets and four times as many social encounters.

The direct transaction between grower and consumer means more personal involvement for both parties. Farmers stand behind their produce literally as they sell it and morally because they grew it. Weak tasting, poor looking vegetables reflect badly on the grower. The customer inspects and turns aside peaches and nectarines in full view of the person who raised them. The customer must react to the offer, "Try one of my peaches." The grower will actively encourage the customer to feel the cantaloupe for hardness, check the color of its webbing, tap it, and have a taste of one that is cut open. This doesn't happen very often in the supermarket where the produce manager is probably not in view, didn't grow any of the produce, and certainly isn't urging anyone to squeeze the fruit or try free samples.

Farmers take pride in bringing in unusual vegetables. They are good advertising since people are curious and ask questions.

To have a few white pumpkins will help the sale of orange pumpkins. Snow peas will help sell tomatoes. Customers appreciate variety and stimulation. While this can be accomplished through strolling musicians or puppet shows, the best way to do it is through food-related activities such as colorful produce and educational displays. The sale of flowers does amazing things to the visual patterning of a market. People walk differently when they carry a bouquet, as if they are showing off something beautiful before an audience.

Community markets located in downtown areas have helped to reduce the exodus of retail shops to the suburbs. People will come downtown to buy real food from real farmers; that lesson has not been lost on storekeepers and chambers of commerce. The Dutin Farmers Market in Syracuse, New York, was established in 1973 to help revitalize the central business dis-

trict. It has been enthusiastically supported by the chamber of commerce ever since. Monty Houston, the first market manager, reported that sales in downtown stores increased from 8-14% on market day. The success of this venture encouraged the city to expand the program to include a free bus service in the downtown district terminating at the market, converting a section of the main shopping street to a pedestrian mall on Saturdays, and making abandoned lots available to garden clubs. The City Parks Department installed picnic tables adjacent to the Dutin site.

Davis, CALIFORNIA

Diane Drier of the Wilkes-Barre, Pennsylvania, Community Development Office overcame reservations of local merchants by pointing out that the farmers market would not sell canned or frozen meats, or out-of-season foods. Local merchants have been pleased with the number of people brought downtown. The same thing happened in Las Cruces, New Mexico, where local merchants, who were originally apprehensive, now solidly support the community market on the downtown mall as a boon to retail trade along the entire mall. Jack Bundy of the Durham, North Carolina, Revitalization Foundation supports the local farmers market "because it pumps a lot of life into our downtown." A survey of shoppers in York, Pennsylvania, indicated that 23% had come downtown to shop at one of the two farmers markets. Development plans for the business district emphasize a connection between the two farm markets through pedestrian paths and parking facilities. The Alpena, Michigan, open air market was begun in 1978 with the goal of bringing people downtown. The market started with twenty-six sellers and gross sales of $4500 and increased to forty-four sellers and $8000 gross per week. This provided a considerable stimulus to the downtown area.

Fair Day is still a big day for downtown merchants in many small Wisconsin towns. Farmers who come to sell also buy. Several farmers markets in Champaign, Illinois, are operated by a non-profit association of

53

storekeepers and property owners whose goals are to create favorable publicity for the business district, to draw people into the area, and to stimulate retail trade. The Kitchener, Ontario, market with its 560 indoor stalls, attracts 20,000 people on a summer Saturday and 13,000 on an off-season Saturday. It is subsidized by the city because it is good for downtown business.

In San Luis Obispo, California, farmers sell their produce in the parking lot of a local supermarket. The manager encouraged this association because it is good for business. Customers who come to buy vegetables once a week still need dairy products, meat, frozen foods, and canned goods from the supermarket a few steps away. The good image of the farmers market rubs off on the surrounding area. A weekly farmers market is held on Fridays in the parking lot of the Bountiful Harvest Fruit Stand in Dixon, California. Both the market manager and the fruitstand operator benefit from this arrangement. Roadside stand operators in Massachusetts report an increase in trade from having their names prominently displayed on sales trucks and handbills distributed at farmers markets. The entire fresh produce industry benefits from increased consumer awareness; people turned on to local fruits and vegetables continue to choose fresh produce wherever they shop.

FRUITS AND VEGIES AT THEIR BEST

5: FRUITS AND VEGIES AT THEIR BEST:

How to Know the Seasons

Ideally, vegetables should come straight from the field to your kitchen. But that's not always possible. Yet there are many clues to a vegetable's freshness and age. It should look fresh and crisp and have no skin punctures, bruises or decay. When selecting, handle with care to prevent bruising. How you store fresh vegetables at home is important. Separate any soft or bruised vegetables from the firm ones before storing. You'll find nearly all green vegetables will stay crisp longer if refrigerated in plastic bags or covered containers. Leafy vegetables which you have washed should be thoroughly drained before storing.

Produce is at its flavor peak and lowest cost when you buy in season. Your local radio and television stations and newspapers often announce when produce is in most plentiful supply in your area as determined by the U.S. Department of Agriculture. As a further help, refer to the chart in the center of this chapter. It shows varying seasons for the most popular produce items. "Peak" indicates the most abundant and usually least expensive periods. "Lowest availability" means a scarcer supply and probably higher prices.

—Patricia Collier
  Castle & Cooke, Inc.

FRUITS

Apples
Select firm, crisp, well-colored apples. Avoid brown spots, shriveled or soft fruit. Buy apples according to their use: Eating — Winesap, Red or Golden Delicious; Cooking — Rhode Island Greening, York or Rome Beauty; Cooking and Eating — McIntosh, Jonathan, Yellow Newton, Stayman. These are just a few of the many varieties available around the country. Ask which apple is the best for your area and your needs.

Apricots
Look for plump, juicy-looking yellow-orange fruit. Ripe apricots should yield to gentle pressure. Avoid dull-looking shriveled or very soft fruit. Ripe apricots should be used immediately. After preparing the fruit, sprinkle with lemon juice or ascorbic-acid mixture to prevent browning.

Avocados

Available most of the year. Avoid dark spots or broken surfaces. Firm avocados should ripen at room temperature in 3 to 5 days. Speed up ripening by storing avocados in a paperbag. The fruit's own gases will help ripen it. They are ready to eat when they yield to gentle pressure on the skin. To serve, cut avocados in half lengthwise to the seed; twist halves apart; remove seed. Peel and slice or chunk, depending on use. If not eaten immediately, sprinkle with lemon juice or a little ascorbic-acid mixture to prevent browning.

Blueberries

Avoid baskets stained with juice or berries that have started to shrivel. Wash blueberries just before you're ready to use them. Serve with sugar and milk over cereal; use in recipes for salads, pies, sauces, ice cream, muffins, desserts or freeze them without washing for later use.

Blackberries and Raspberries

Select plump, fresh-appearing, uniformly colored fruit. Berries should be free of stems or leaves. Blackberries should be black; if red they are not ripe. Avoid stained baskets. Wash berries just before use. Water causes mold.

Cherries

Look for plump, bright-appearing cherries with color ranging from light to bright red to purplish-black, depending on the variety you're selecting. Tart or sour cherries cook up best. Sweet cherries can be eaten fresh or used in cooking. Avoid overly soft or shriveled fruit or dark-colored stems. All indicate cherries past their prime.

Coconuts

Shake a few. Buy the one with the most liquid, but not if it's leaking. After you've drained the liquid by puncturing the "eyes", heat in a 350°F oven about 30 minutes (until shell cracks) to get the meat from the shell. It will open easily and the flesh will have separated from the shell. Or, you can put it in the freezer for an hour or two. The brittle shell will then crack with one hammer blow.

Cranberries

Bad cranberries are rare because inferior berries ordinarily are sorted out before they're packed. Avoid shriveled, discolored or moist cranberries. Wash before using. Water causes spotting. Cranberries can be kept 4 to 8 weeks in your refrigerator. Or you can freeze them in their package for later use.

Grapes

Plump and firm with green stems means grapes are at their best. A good color for the variety being offered usually means good flavor. Avoid dry, brittle stems, shriveled grapes or bunches with small undeveloped grapes.

Grapefruit

Varieties available include those with seeds or without seeds, with pink flesh or white flesh. They're all good. Taste-test to choose your favorite. Select well-shaped, firm but springy-to-the-touch fruit that's heavy for its size. Smooth, thin-skinned grapefruit is usually juiciest. Avoid fruit that has a pointed end or is soft and puffy.

Kiwis

This little fruit has a wonderful, delicate strawberry-like taste. Squeeze one very gently to check ripeness; it should give a little. Peel off the furry skin and eat the fruit plain or in a fruit salad. It's also delicious when sliced onto yogurt or ice cream.

Lemons

For the best buy, look for bright, firm lemons, heavy for their size with fine-textured skin. Rough lemons have thicker skins and less juice. A slight greenish cast means the juice will be more acid. Check the stem end for signs of aging or decay.

Limes

Firm, glossy-skinned limes are best. They should be heavy for their size. Brown spots do not affect quality. They'll keep longer when refrigerated. Avoid yellow-skinned, dry or hard limes.

NOTE: The ascorbic acid in lemons and limes will keep sliced peaches, apples and bananas from turning brown. It also adds sprightly flavor to most soft fruits.

Melons

Melons don't increase in sugar or sweetness after they're picked, but do become riper and more mellow. Chill melons to preserve their "peak of flavor". Use these guidelines when selecting varieties:

CANTALOUPES — Select cantaloupes having a fine beige netting on the rind. The stem end should be smooth and yield slightly to the touch.

PERSIAN MELONS — Larger and rounder than cantaloupes, the Persians also have a finer netting. Choose as you would cantaloupes.

CRENSHAW MELONS — Large (up to 9 pounds) with rounded blossom ends and pointed stem ends. They should be golden, have lengthwise ribbing and no netting. They have a juicy, rich, spicy taste.

CASABA MELONS — Their ribbing is very definite and the skin is rich golden-yellow. A slight springiness when you press the blossom end means the melon is ripe.

HONEYDEW MELONS — These should have a yellowish to creamy-white color and a soft, velvety feel. Rind should be slightly soft around the blossom end.

Nectarines

Select firm, plump fruit, wellformed and slightly soft along the seam. Color will be reddish to yellowish, depending on variety. Slightly firm fruit should ripen well at room temperature. Avoid hard, soft or shriveled fruit. Green nectarines will shrivel instead of ripening.

Oranges

Firm oranges, heavy for their size are the best buy. Blemishes or scars don't affect the fruit inside. Navel and Temple oranges are easily peeled and sectioned. Valencia, Parson Brown, Pineapple and Hamlin varieties have abundant juice. Navel oranges are seedless, Hamlins and Valencias have very few seeds. Avoid dry, soft or spongy fruit.

Papayas

Choose papayas with at least 35% spreckled yellow skin. These will ripen completely in 2 to 3 days at room temperature. A papaya should have a fruity aroma and yield slightly to pressure. Avoid those with dark spots or any that show wetness when gently pressed on the stem end.

Peaches

The main difference between the two top grades of peaches is their color; more blush on the U.S. Fancy grade and a yellow or creamy color for the U.S. Choice. Look for fairly firm to slightly softened fruit. Avoid green, shriveled or bruised fruit. When selecting peaches use your nose!

Pears

Pears are ripe when they yield readily to soft pressure in the palm of the hand. Ripen firm pears at room temperature. Avoid shriveled, discolored, cut or bruised fruit. Select Bartlett, Anjou, and Bosc pears for eating fresh and for cooking. Comice, Secke, Nelis, Kieffer are best for eating fresh.

Plums

Try different varieties for a nice taste change. Look for plump fruit that yields to gentle pressure on the skin and is well colored for the variety being offered. Plum colors will vary from bright yellow-green to reddish-purple to purplish-black. Avoid hard, shriveled or soft plums and ones with cracks or sunburn marks.

Strawberries

Full red color, uniformly shaped berries with stem cap still attached are best. Avoid dull or shrunken berries or leaky ones indicated by stained containers.

Watermelon

Look for a velvety bloom on the rind. The underbelly, where it has rested on the ground should be yellowish or amber, not stark white or greenish. Ripeness is difficult to determine. Your best buy is to purchase in halves or quarters. Flesh should be firm and of good red color. Seeds should be dark brown. Avoid melons with a hard white streak running through the edible flesh.

VEGETABLES

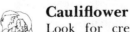

Broccoli

Stalks should be tender and firm with compact heads of a dark or purplish-green. Yellow buds mean the vegetable is too mature. Broccoli is a good source of vitamins, iron, potassium and riboflavin. Very few calories. Cook to tender-crisp, never soft.

Artichokes

Look for compact, plump artichokes, heavy for their size, with tightly closed, thick, green, blemish-free leaves. Rub one against the other. If they squeak, they're fresh. Size is not an indication of quality.

Brussels Sprouts

Look for firm, compact and bright green sprouts. Never yellow. Before cooking slice a little off the butt end — not so much that leaves fall off. Cut an X in the stem so they cook quickly. To prevent a cabbage smell as they cook, put a walnut in the pot. It will cut down the cooking odor.

Asparagus

Look for firm, straight stalks with tightly closed tips. The young, slim stalks are usually considered the most tender. Avoid wilted, limp, flat or angular stalks — they're usually tough and stringy. Before cooking, snap off the white ends with your hands. They break easily near the edible part.

Cabbage

Red and green cabbages should be firm and feel heavy for their size. Color should be bright. Cabbage can be stored in your crisper in a plastic bag for weeks. Use for coleslaw, salads, pickled vegetables, sauerkraut or serve it hot with or without seasonings.

Beans

To buy green or wax beans, look for crisp but tender beans without scars. They should have a pliable, velvety feel, not hard or tough. Well-shaped pods with small seeds are desirable. Length is unimportant. To clean, rinse in cold water. Snap off ends and pull out "string".

Carrots

Look for firm, well-shaped, fresh-looking carrots. If stem ends are discolored, the carrots are too mature. The good carrot taste comes from the bright orange core where sugar is stored.

Beets

Small beets are young and tender; large ones can be tough and woody. The roots should be smooth and firm, not soft, and the tops should look fresh. Never cut or peel beets before cooking — their color and nutrition will bleed away in the cooking water.

Cauliflower

Look for creamy-white, compact, tightly packed flowerets without smudges. Leaves around base should be fresh and green. Cauliflower is delicious raw, in salads, creamed or steamed with butter and seasonings.

Celery

Celery should appear fresh, crisp, clean and of medium length and size. Pale green in color. Thin dark-green stalks may be stringy. Celery adds flavor to soups, stews and casseroles. It's excellent raw, stir fried and in salads.

Corn

Select medium-size corn ears with bright green husks. Pull the husk down an inch or so to be sure the ear displays plump, milky, tender kernels. Tiny kernels indicate corn is too young. Large, deep yellow kernels are tough.

Cucumbers

The perfect cucumber is long, lean, well shaped with good green color. Overmature cucumbers are generally seedy, dull or yellow and have an overgrown, puffy look. The European or English cucumber is a new type on the market. It's seedless and less bitter than the regular variety, but greenhouse grown — making it more expensive. The waxy preservative on cucumbers is harmless. It can be scrubbed or peeled off.

Eggplant

Be sure eggplants are firm, with a shiny rich purple color and a bright green cap. They should appear heavy for their size. Avoid scars or bruises. Wrinkled or flabby eggplant will usually be bitter-tasting.

Lettuce

Remember the softer the lettuce, the sooner you should use it. First cut off the butt end, then rinse, blot with paper towels and store lettuce in plastic in the crisper. Never store lettuce next to apples, plums, bananas, pears, avocados, tomatoes or melons. These fruits give off ethylene gas which can spot lettuce.

There are many varieties of lettuce each having its own special texture and flavor. Salads take on excitement when you use two or three different types. Some popular varieties are: Iceberg, Romaine, Butter or Cobb, Boston, Bibb and Celtuce. Experiment!

Mushrooms

As mushrooms mature they lose moisture. This gradually causes their veils to open. Open or closed, the veils do not affect the mushroom's quality. Open veils bring out a full-bodied flavor. Closed veil mushrooms have a lighter, more delicate flavor. Select to fit your tastes.

Sizes vary. Select to fit your use. Small for salads, garnishes or sauces. Medium for serving raw with dips or sauteing. Large for stuffing or broiling.

Onions

Select clean, firm onions with dry, brittle skin. The best times to buy are — Bermudas in March, Spanish in August and Red Torpedos only in the early summer. Don't store onions and potatoes together. The moisture potatoes give off can rot or help sprout onions.

continued p. 64

Buy in seaso[n]

	PEAK TO GOOD		FAIR		LOW TO NOT AVAILABLE

Fruits	JAN	FEB	MAR	APR	MAY	JUN	JUL	AUG	SEP	OCT	NOV
APPLES											
APRICOTS											
AVOCADOS											
BANANAS											
BLACKBERRIES RASPBERRIES											
BLUEBERRIES											
CANTALOUPES											
CHERRIES											
COCONUTS											
CRANBERRIES											
GRAPEFRUIT											
GRAPES											
HONEYDEW MELONS											
KIWIS											
LEMONS											
LIMES											
NECTARINES											
ORANGES											
PAPAYAS											
PEACHES											
PEARS											
PINEAPPLES											
PLUMS											
STRAWBERRIES											
WATERMELONS											

Source: United Fresh Fruit and Vegetable Ass[ociation]

r flavor and savings

getables	JAN	FEB	MAR	APR	MAY	JUN	JUL	AUG	SEP	OCT	NOV	DEC
TICHOKES												
ARAGUS												
ANS, GREEN												
ETS												
OCCOLI												
SSELS OUTS												
BBAGE												
RROTS												
ULIFLOWER												
LERY												
RN, SWEET												
CUMBERS												
GPLANT												
TTUCE												
SHROOMS												
ONS												
ONS, GREEN												
SLEY												
S, GREEN												
PPERS												
ATOES												
DISHES												
NACH												
UASH												
ET TOES												
MATOES												
RNIPS												
ERCRESS												

Green Onions/ Scallions

Bunches with fresh, crisp, green tops and medium sized necks are best. They're mild all year round. They're also very fragile so refrigerate in the crisper. Don't forget to use the green stems, as well as the bulb, in salads and for cooking.

Parsley

Several varieties are available, including garden variety and the more flavorful Italian, broad leaf and Cilantro (Mexican or Chinese parsley). Garden variety is used mainly for garnish. Parsley should have bright coloring and look fresh.

Peas

Small pods mean tender peas. Be sure they're fresh. Fresh peas should squeak when pods are rubbed together. Refrigerate unshelled. Serve as soon as possible.

Bell Peppers

Peppers that are firm, shiny and thick-fleshed, medium to dark green or bright red are your best buy. Avoid wilted or flabby peppers and ones with cuts or punctures.

Potatoes

Look for firm, solid ones without sprouts. Green areas mean the potatoes have been exposed to light too long. Store potatoes in a cool, dry place. Never in your refrigerator. There are many varieties. Best for baking are Russet Burbank, Green Mountain, White Rose and Kennebec. For boiling and other cooking methods look for Katahdin, Cobbler or Triumph.

Radishes

Uniformly shaped radishes that are free of blemishes, firm and bright, deep red or white (depending upon variety) are the best buys. Discard tops and wash before refrigerating.

Spinach

Crisp, dark green in color with no yellowish leaves means spinach is fresh. Rinse carefully in cold water, trim and discard the stems. Use as soon as possible for best retention of flavor and nutrients.

Squash (summer variety)

Pattypan, Straightneck or Crookneck, Zucchini and Italian Marrow are best if selected medium sized with very tender rinds. Avoid soft areas. Do not overcook. Serve crisply cooked.

Squash (winter variety)

Acorn, Banana, Butternut, Des Moines, Green and Golden Delicious, Green and Blue Hubbard are some examples of Winter Squash. Bake or steam this type of squash with the shell on. The large center seeds should be scraped out before cooking.

Sweet Potatoes/
and Yams

For quality, select small or medium-sized ones free of cracks or damp areas. They're best if they taper at both ends. Yams are sweeter, deeper orange and more moist than sweet potatoes.

Tomatoes

Size does not indicate quality. Look for firm, unblemished tomatoes with good color. If you're buying them to eat another day, select pale pink ones and ripen them at home. Tiny cherry tomatoes are very perishable and should be used at once.

Turnips

Select firm, unblemished turnips, heavy for their size, with fresh tops. Serve sliced, chunked, mashed or in soups and stews. Use tops for salad greens or as a cooked vegetable.

Watercress

Look for crisp, bright green leaves. To store, wash and wrap in plastic and place in crisper. To rejuvenate, snip off ends and place in water in your refrigerator.

6: SOME TYPICAL AND SOME UNUSUAL MARKETS

Each farmers market has its own personality based on local geography and culture. This quickly becomes evident to the sellers who know that shoppers in City A are primarily interested in quality while those in nearby B are chiefly concerned with prices, and in C they want specialty foods. Some cities are good places to sell dried fruits while at others customers won't look at them. There are walking distance markets such as those in New York City and automobile markets such as those in San Francisco. The market in my own city has a lot of bicycle shoppers. Some markets are in a totally enclosed building, such as that owned by the farmers in South Bend, Indiana; others such as the bustling West Allis, Wisconsin, market have covered sheds with open sides; some downtown sellers use beach umbrellas or canvas covers donated by local merchants; and most of the smaller trade days and courthouse sales are strictly open-air operations.

Springfield, ILLINOIS

Fayetteville, ARKANSAS

Typical Markets

The Good Food Cooperative has been the guiding spirit of the community market in Moscow, Idaho, for over five years. The growers are all small operators, producing exclusively for direct sales or for personal consumption. A forty-mile radius is the limit from which growers can truck in produce. This allows sellers to come from eastern Washington as well as from some excellent garden areas southeast of Moscow. According to the organizers, market prices are consistently lower than at supermarkets for 90% of the items. Most customers are regulars who attend at least ten markets during the July-October season.

The Rural Mountain Producers' Exchange is held in the town square of Fayetteville, Arkansas, on Saturday mornings and also on Tuesday and Thursday mornings during the peak growing season. The exchange operates five or six months of the year and closes down during the winter months. It began in 1974 with a grant from the local Economic Opportunity Agency and has since become self-supporting. Members (sellers) pay a $5 yearly membership charge and a 10% commission on all sales. In 1979 there were 105 members. The Exchange is governed by a seven-person Board of Directors and hires a paid manager. Members are restricted to selling locally produced goods. No home baked or canned goods may be sold and no scales are used. These rules were established to avoid conflict with county and state authorities. The market is healthy and has been growing at a rate of 20-30% a year.

An attempt in the 1960s to revive a farmers market in downtown Springfield, Illinois, failed badly. The first session attracted two farmers and six customers. This depressing state continued for four weeks before the organizers gave up. Two years later another attempt was made with similar meager results. In 1970 a third attempt was undertaken, and this time there were intense preparations in contacting growers in the area. A representative from the Springfield Central Development Association visited meetings of farmers and wrote personal letters. Affirmative replies of support were received from twelve growers. This seemed enough for a beginning. On opening day, three showed up but they sold out within ten minutes. The organizers saw that this event was given a great deal of publicity in the local press. The second week, ten farmers came and they sold out within twenty minutes. This was also given considerable media attention, along with assurances to the public that there would be more farmers coming the following week. The hopes of the organizers were realized, and publicity attracted more farmers and more customers. The market caught hold and has operated successfully ever since.

Eugene, Oregon, is a progressive university city with a reputation for local initiative. Located in the bountiful Willamette Valley, Eugene would seem an excellent place for a farmers market. However, a search during

Syracuse, NEW YORK

a visit in 1978 proved frustrating. I was directed first to a converted warehouse which enclosed restaurants, coffee shops, craft displays, a good fish market, and one produce stall which sold some local items in season. The manager of the produce stand directed me to the Saturday Market held on the downtown mall. This proved to be an excellent outlet for local arts and crafts but did not make the grade as a farmers market. Oregonians have traditionally patronized fruit stands, many of which have a regular clientele, and families are used to driving to the country for their fruits and vegetables. However, the gas shortage is changing this. Fewer cars on the road has meant the closing of some roadside stands. Customers as well as farmers soon realized that a farmers market might be a suitable alternative and, during the summer of 1979, an attempt was made to revive the Eugene market. Several Sunday sessions

Syracuse, NEW YORK

were held at the county fairgrounds. The first one in June drew more customers than the seven farmers could handle. This kind of imbalance is typical during the formative years of a new retail outlet. Either there are too many customers and not enough farmers or vice versa. Later in the summer the market was moved into a one-block site adjacent to the well-established Saturday crafts market in the downtown district.

The success of the Dutin Farmers Market begun in 1973 in Syracuse, New York, has already been mentioned. The city supports it by assigning police for security, providing occasional entertainment through the Department of Parks and Recreation, and using employees from the Department of Public Works to set up street barricades and clean up afterwards. City and county agencies and community organizations use the market for public information programs. The county library may be there with its bookmobile and the fire department with a prevention exhibit. Ten of the fifty-six spaces are ordinarily occupied by dealers who purchase at the wholesale market, the remaining forty-six spaces are reserved for farmers who grow and sell their own crops. It is the belief of the market manager that having dealers present is necessary in order to provide consumers with a sufficient variety of produce. Most spaces are rented for the entire season; farmers pay $60 a year, dealers $150. Besides the downtown market, there is a second direct produce outlet in Syracuse in conjunction with the Central New York State Regional Produce Market. This contains sheds for 340 farmers and open selling aisles able to accommodate an additional 200 farmers. Two sheds are heated and can be used during the winter months.

Seattle's Pike Place Market started in 1907 as a revolt on the part of producers and consumers against their "common enemy —the middleman." The market flourished during the depression when it was the cheapest place to buy vegetables. If one came late in the day when the farmers sought to sell at any price rather than truck the produce home, prices were even lower. Sales were dealt a severe blow in 1942 when most Japanese were forcibly evacuated from the West Coast, since almost two-thirds of those selling at the market were Japanese truck gardeners. Following the Second World War, urban sprawl took over much of the land that the small growers had used. Taxes for the remaining farmers skyrocketed as their land was zoned for commercial-industrial use. Public transit to the market declined and people left the central city for the suburbs. By 1956 the city was about to give up its lease on the market and replace it with a grand development scheme for the area. A group of local citizens calling themselves "Friends of the Market" circulated an initiative petition to preserve and restore the market which was finally passed by the voters in 1971.

Pennsylvania's seventy-five farm markets are a mixed bag. Some like the Green Dragon in Ephrata are enormous operations containing several hundred stalls selling everything from appliances to ice cream. Some are largely flea markets or auction galleries, but all sell local produce in season. The Downingtown Farmers Market is a huge building, four football fields in length, which attracts more than 40,000 customers on a typical weekend using such promotional devices as an indoor trout stream, country concerts, and car shows. The Quakertown Farmers Market contains an art gallery, antique and flea market, a tobacco stall not to be confused with the nearby rope shop, a barber shop, and a seafood snackery.

New York City's first Greenmarket began on a dirt lot on 59th Street in East Manhattan. Opening day brought only four vegetable growers, two house plant sellers, and an egg seller. The response from the waiting public was overwhelming. Media coverage attracted more farmers, and within a month's time all eighteen selling stalls were occupied. The Greenmarket was sponsored by the Council on the Environment of New York City, a nonprofit group dedicated to improving life in the city. It was the brainchild of architect Barry Benepe who saw it as a means of halting the destruction of farmland surrounding New York City and of getting fresh vegetables on the tables of city residents.

Unlike small town trade days which can be started on a shoestring, anything in New York City requires time and money. Getting the markets organized was a frustrating business since it involved the jurisdiction of a half dozen city agencies and consultation with community planning boards and business organizations, as well as donations from six foundations. In 1979 Greenmarkets were operating at eleven sites around the city. While municipal officials are publicly enthusiastic about the program, little has been done to translate this into tangible support. Initially the Greenmarket organizers were charged only $1 a year for the use of a city-owned lot. Because of the continuing fiscal crisis, city officials have proposed that this fee be raised to $650. The 59th Street location is currently threatened by the planned construction of a twenty-five story office building.

In 1972, two Japanese writers who visited farmers markets around the world, commented on the inappropriateness of such an operation for New York City. "For instance," they wrote, "if a primitive, outdoor market opened in an empty lot in Manhattan, it would be of little use to the people in the Manhattan area, who have ready access to other facilities." This was written several years before the first "primitive outdoor market" opened on East 59th Street. If these observers could visit one of New York's eleven Greenmarkets now, they would find great similarities between the activities of ordinary people buying fresh fruits and vegetables for table use and what they saw at marketplaces around the world.

At the other end of the country in Los Angeles, a farmers market was started in 1934, when trucks laden with fruits and vegetables grown in the surrounding area pulled into what was then a huge dirt parking lot and sold their freshly picked produce to local residents. Although today the trucks are gone, the quality remains, and the atmosphere is still that of a "farmers market." Agriculture has ceased to be a leading industry in the Los Angeles basin today, mainly because of the smog and great distances between locations which make travel costs for the small farmer prohibitive. L.A. county crop losses due to smog were estimated at $2,900,000 in 1970.

Another community market was started in 1979 in Gardena in a church parking lot. It was organized by the Interfaith Hunger Coalition, a church-related group which hired a twenty-year-old student as its manager. Of the ten growers selling at the market on a July Saturday, none came from Los Angeles. All had driven considerable distances, some over 100 miles. A few were selling combined loads from several neighboring farms. This was made possible by a change in the 1979 state regulations establishing certificated farm markets in California which allowed one certified producer to sell for two certified producers. Without this change, it would not be economically feasible for a single grower to drive long distances to sell half a truckload of oranges or melons.

Unusual Markets

The chief business of the private sales barn in Moorefield, West Virginia, is selling livestock, but the owner-auctioneer will also sell produce in season to enliven the market and as a service to customers. The Paterson, New Jersey, Farmers Market is basically a wholesale terminal that deals in bulk sales but there is also a lively retail trade in season. The Paterson Market began during the depression as a salesplace for small farmers. At its peak, more than 300 growers came every evening to sell produce. During the Second World War, direct sales to customers dropped and the number of participating growers dwindled to twenty-five or thirty. However, in recent years, rising food prices have awakened consumer interests in direct sales. Also in New Jersey, the Trenton Farmers Market was constructed by the farmers themselves following the Second World War. The building is in the shape of an X, with the market manager seated at the card table at the axis and trucks backed up to stalls along the arms. The market sells mostly specialty ethnic foods during the winter months—Italian and Latvian bread, bok choy, Chinese parsley, black mushrooms, pierogi, and prosciutto, but as soon as the local growing season begins, the ethnic foods are lost in an explosion of apples, pears, berries, Jersey tomatoes, and six varieties of sweet corn.

The Tomales Bay, California, Vegetable Swap has operated for several years on a barter basis. It began as several tables in front of City Hall on Friday mornings where home gardeners could exchange produce. No money was traded when the swap began. A box of squash was exchanged for a crate of melons or peaches. Soon non-gardeners wanted a piece of the action and brought in baked goods, homemade jams and jellies, and local fishing people brought in their surplus catch, mostly rock cod and Tomales Bay shrimp.

The entire operation takes place in little more than an hour every Friday morning. The event is publicized with fliers run off in the local school and left in stores, offices, and community buildings.

Farmers markets in several Wisconsin cities are held in conjunction with flea markets which sell second-hand goods. Some of these markets attract 10-20,000 people on a summer Saturday. The Ontario Department of Highways has helped to establish four farmers markets along Queen Elizabeth Way for the sole use of growers in the area who lost their roadside stands when the highway was constructed.

West Oakland, CALIFORNIA

7: HOW TO START A COMMUNITY MARKE

To make a rabbit stew, first catch the rabbit. To create a farm market, first catch the farmers; the rest comes later. In large urban areas, farmers have been pushed out to the periphery as their former land has been devoured by development. Those who remain already have outlets for their crops or they would not survive. You can obtain a list from your county extension agent of those farmers who operate or supply roadside stands. You can also contact the growers listed on a farm trails map or those who run U-pick operations. Such farmers already have experience selling directly to the public and are likely to be sympathetic to the idea of a community marketplace. Some organizers have found it useful to give talks at the county grange and send personal letters to small growers in the area.

The next challenge is to get an initial group signed up. Many small growers are fiercely independent and won't want to commit themselves in advance to a formal organization. Fortunately it is not necessary to recruit a large number of growers in order to begin. The first New York City Greenmarket drew four farm sellers on opening day, and the Philadelphia Tailgate Market Program began in 1977 with six growers selling to consumers from the backs of trucks.

Accounts of successful markets elsewhere can help convince local farmers to join in. There are useful films, slide packets, and published accounts of successful markets around the country (see list of sources in Appendix). The strongest sales pitch will come from small growers who already sell profitably at community markets in other locations.

Most towns have found that a small group of suppliers is sufficient to start a new market. Once it begins operating, recruitment of additional farmers will be easier. The existence of an outlet will encourage gardeners to expand their operations and others, who always wanted to farm, may lease a few acres. The latter group will include both young people holding other jobs who want to work the land and older people who would like the extra income and challenge of a small commercial growing operation. However, you cannot depend on suppliers who have not yet begun farming. The first participants must be people already growing crops and the best prospects will be those who already sell directly to the public.

A single strong grower with a diversified operation can carry a market for several years until it becomes established. This person has to be someone like Ervin Geils of Des Plaines, Illinois, or Vance Corum of Gardena, California. At my local market, a retired couple, Ed and Virginia Looney, carried things along through the early years, particularly during the bleak winter months when no one else would sell in the

rain or cold wind. The Looneys typically offer more than twenty different items, including some from their cold storage locker.

An organizing committee and sponsors are necessary. This was not the case in colonial times when markets were simple associations of growers who rented a plot of land in the city and developed their own rules. Now there are so many regulations and city agencies to be consulted that small farmers would have difficulty doing this themselves and still growing crops. Securing testimonials from chambers of commerce will assist in gaining business support and head off potential opposition later. A municipal agency such as a planning department or recreation department may become sponsors. In Redmond, Washington, the Saturday Market was the inspiration of the head gardener of the city park who was searching for new ways to contact people with plant problems. She imagined that a farmers market might be a good place to offer advice, and ever since the market was established in 1975, she has been there giving free gardening service. Garden clubs are also potential sponsors as well as sources of produce. In low income neighborhoods, look to church groups and activist organizations for support.

At this point, you've got a dozen farmers signed up, an organizing committee, and a list of sponsors. The next objective is a location. You need a place accessible to the public with adequate parking and public transportation. One approach is to find vacant city-owned land or the parking lot of some organization such as a church that is not in use on Saturday mornings. An advantage of holding Philadelphia Tailgate Markets in church parking lots and church school yards has been that the insurance carried by the churches covers all activities taking place in these locations.

Finding a site will require consultation with city officials, business leaders, and community organizations. This process will generate community interest. A neighborhood that has been involved in the development of a market will be likely to support it afterwards. The Stockton, California, market is located under a busy freeway. It is noisy and aesthetically unattractive, but it is highly accessible, has good parking, and the customers come in droves. Some of the best-established markets on the East Coast and in the Midwest have been operating continuously for over a century in courthouse squares. These locations have high visibility, are well known to local residents, and are usually more attractive than vacant lots. Other possible locations are in city or county parks, or you might induce the city to close a street once a week. This involves considerable red tape, but it can be done, especially if storekeepers view the market as a boon to business. A downtown shopping mall may be the right location provided there is good access for the farm trucks.

Funding won't be a serious problem in a small town if the sponsoring organizations are willing to donate supplies and do the paperwork. In some communities the county extension agent will help organize the market and make office supplies and facilities available. A downtown merchants' association may also be willing to contribute time and personnel to get the program started. The situation is more complicated in large cities where there is more red tape and expense. The New York City Greenmarket Program received grants from six private foundations totaling in excess of $60,000 and still depends on grants to cover administrative costs. If you need outside funding to get started, a good bet would be a service organization which would adopt the market as its yearly project or a local foundation dedicated to civic improvement. A directory of foundations is available in your local library. You can also turn to your state department of agriculture for technical assistance and possibly a start-up grant. Many states have special programs to encourage direct farm sales. A county agent will have access to all these programs as well as a virtually unlimited supply of pamphlets on food production and consumption.

Once you've acquired the necessary funding to start your market, a paid manager can be hired. This is an individual responsible for handling all the details, including health and safety regulations, lease agreements on the property, insurance, etc. The first manager should be someone with boundless energy and a willingness to work hard for little money. The goals of the farmers market are something to which most people can commit themselves with enthusiasm. However, enthusiasm by itself isn't enough. Skills at organizing people and working with city authorities will be essential. At the outset, it will be a seven-day-a-week job recruiting farmers, working with city and county officials, gaining the support of local merchants, acquiring the necessary funds, and obtaining publicity. Once the market is established, the job routine will take only one or two days a week.

The next step is to find people who want to eat "rabbit stew." Publicity! That's the way to reach consumers. Whenever there is a newspaper account about our local market, attendance rises. Most newspapers regard a farmers market as a newsworthy enterprise. It's loaded with human interest and good picture possibilities. Having a televi-

sion crew film opening day will draw customers the following week and encourage additional farmers to participate. Paid newspaper ads and radio commercials

Ithaca, NEW YORK

haven't proven very successful yet. You will be better off with free feature articles and public service announcements if you can get them. The best advertising for direct sales is word of mouth. Markets have attempted to capitalize on this through the sale of tee-shirts, bumper stickers, aprons, and shopping bags containing a market emblem. Posters and notices can be placed at various community gathering places. Contests and prizes will generate publicity. A ribbon or small cash award can be given for the largest pumpkin, the longest ear of corn, the most interesting shaped potato, and the fuzziest peach. Prizes can also be given for the most creative recipe for an unusual vegetable such as kale or chard. Festivals and concerts will attract public attention. For the thirty-sixth anniversary of the San Francisco Farmers Market there were strolling musicians, cooking and canning demonstrations, a beauty queen crowned with a wreath of garlic by the mayor, and a "farmer of the year" award for the oldest grower actively selling.

Following regulations is easier in practice than in theory. The actual problems that have arisen in regards to insurance, sanitation, or certification rules have been more hypothetical than real. There was no category for "farmers market" in the price manual used by insurance brokers in our area. Their first inclination was to charge the rates applied to a county fair or concert. This would have resulted in excessive costs and full-time coverage during the season. Discussion of these issues with several insurance brokers resulted in one firm's coming up with an attractively low rate structure. The county agricultural agent can be very helpful in identifying relevant regulations.

Stall rentals should reflect market needs.

These may be used to favor local producers, senior citizens or young people's organizations such as scouts or 4H. Differential rentals may also be used to encourage certain products. The Kitchener, Ontario, sales area charges $35 a year for fruit and vegetable stands inside the building, $100 for fish stalls, and $200 for meat sales. Selling directly from the back of a truck outdoors costs $75 a year. San Francisco's market has both a daily and an annual rate for covered stalls and a lower rate for outside truck bed sales. Detroit's Eastern Farmers Market segregates dealers selling wholesale produce from genuine farmers. Dealers are placed on the opposite side of the aisles and typically given the less desirable stalls. It has been the policy of the market manager to limit the number of dealers who sell items that might be competitive with farmers.

Once the market becomes established, new needs will arise. The organizing committee can be replaced by an administrative board that makes policies and sets stall fees. It is desirable to obtain consumer representation on the board. This will keep the market from becoming isolated from the community. Most markets jealously protect their informality and try to keep rules to a minimum. Some hold town meetings at the end of the selling day. Signs are placed throughout the site inviting growers and customers to attend. This is a good way to keep problems from becoming serious.

Now you've got your farmers, your customers, an efficient and energetic manager, a supportive city administration, interested downtown merchants, a minimum set of rules, and a decision-making procedure. That's it. You have all it takes for a successful community market!

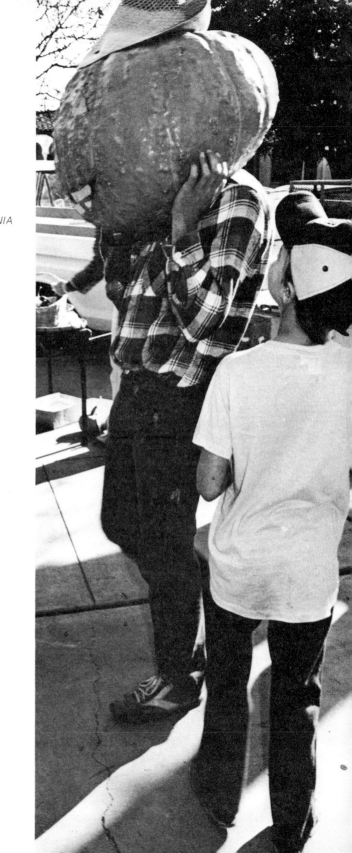

Davis, CALIFORNIA

8: THE VEGIE REVOLUTION COOKBOOK

Poorly cooked vegetables cannot be properly appreciated. There should be a law against overcooking vegetables; soggy peas or mealy carrots are a crime against nature. Cooking times given in recipe books are only estimates because some varieties of certain vegetables will cook faster than others. Some stoves cook more quickly than others and there may even be one burner on your stove that gets hotter than the others.

As a good cook's prerogative, you may want to taste the vegetables as they cook, but always remove them from the stove when they are still crisp and firm. Remember, the critical interval during which a green vegetable is "just right" lasts only a few minutes. If you are lucky enough to get fresh, flavorful, *farmers market* produce, you will certainly appreciate the care that goes into fine preparations of vegetables.

Red Sunflower Hash

Serves 2 or 3

2 small raw beets
1 large carrot
1 large red or white onion
4 T wheat germ (if available)
½ t caraway seeds
½ C sunflower seeds
2 eggs slightly beaten
2 T oil
2 T parmesan cheese

Chop finely by hand or in a food processor the beets, carrot, and onion to a hash-like consistency. Add wheat germ, sunflower seeds, and caraway seeds. Stir in lightly beaten eggs and mix well. Heat oil in a skillet. Turn hash into skillet and scramble over medium heat for 7 minutes or until eggs are well cooked and hash is not runny. Top with parmesan cheese and serve as a main course or side dish.

Squash Blossoms

These are the infertile male blossoms of the squash plant. They can be sauteed very lightly in butter for 1 minute and served by themselves as a vegetable dish, or included with eggs in an omelet. The blossoms can also be stuffed with chopped mushrooms and celery, or chopped chicken and chopped celery and heated until warm. Do not overcook.

Chinese Cabbage* with Dill

Serves 3 or 4

*Also called Napa cabbage

½ cabbage head thinly sliced
2 T butter or margarine
¼ C water
1 T lemon juice
1 t dill
salt to taste

Slice cabbage and stir-fry in the butter or margarine. Add water, cook covered for 5 minutes. When still crunchy to the teeth, add lemon juice, dill, and salt to taste. Serve warm. Do not overcook.

Gratin de Choux
A light custard side dish

Serves 4-6

1 bunch broccoli, asparagus, or cauliflower, cut into 1-inch pieces

Sauce:

2 C milk or half and half
3 slightly beaten eggs
½ C grated swiss or jack cheese
½ t nutmeg
½ t salt
⅛ t pepper (white if available)

Boil or steam vegetables until they are just barely tender. Arrange on the bottom of a lightly greased 9 x 13 inch baking dish. Lightly mix sauce ingredients together with a fork and pour over vegetables. Bake in a preheated 300° oven for 40 minutes.

Ted's Winter Vegetables and Sizzling Rice

Feeds 3 normal people or 2 surfers

1½ C brown or white rice
2 T oil
3 C water
1 T cooking sherry (optional)
1 T soy sauce
1 onion, diced
2 large carrots, sliced
1 stalk broccoli, sliced
1 leek or 2 stalks celery sliced
1 C grated cheese
½ C sour cream
salt and pepper to taste

Heat oil in large frying pan until water drops will dance across its surface. Pour in rice and cook over medium heat while stirring constantly. Add water, soy sauce, and sherry. Don't be startled by the sizzle. It's supposed to do this. Cover pan and reduce heat to low. After 5 minutes, place vegetables on top of the rice. Allow everything to simmer (still covered) for another 15 minutes or until all the liquid has cooked away. Add salt and pepper to taste. Sprinkle on the grated cheese and allow it to melt. Serve immediately with optional sour cream.

Isla Vista Stuffed Peppers

Serves 4 as a side dish and 2 as a main course

1½ C rice
3 C water
3 fresh tomatoes, cut into sections, or 1 16-ounce can of stewed tomatoes
4 large green bell peppers
1½ C grated jack cheese
½ C chopped walnuts or almonds
1½ t curry powder
parsley or dill (optional)

With fresh tomatoes, cook them along with rice. With stewed tomatoes, cook rice in liquid from the tomato can, and then add the tomatoes after the rice has finished. Boil or steam rice in water for 20 minutes (until all water has been absorbed). Add nuts, jack cheese, curry powder, salt and pepper. Blanch the bell peppers by dropping them into boiling water for 5 minutes, then quickly transferring them into cold water. Stuff the peppers with the rice mixture and top with the remaining cheese. Place stuffed peppers in a baking dish or broiler pan and run under a broiler *briefly* until the cheese is melted. Sprinkle with a garnish parsley or dill if desired. Serve immediately.

Eggplant Lasagne

Serves 4

1 medium eggplant
⅔ C bread crumbs
1 T parmesan cheese
½ clove garlic, crushed
½ t each oregano, basil, and marjoram
2 C tomato sauce
1 C sliced mushrooms
1 T butter
1 C grated cheese (jack, mozzarella, or cheddar)

Preheat oven to 400°. Peel eggplant and slice into one-third inch slices. Place eggplant slices in a greased 9 x 13 inch baking pan. Combine bread crumbs, garlic, parmesan, and spices and sprinkle over eggplant slices. Bake for about 20 minutes or until eggplant is tender. Pour tomato sauce over eggplant. Saute mushrooms in 1 T butter and place on top of tomato sauce. Sprinkle grated cheese on top and bake until heated through and cheese is melted.

Winter Salad

Winter presents a challenge for the salad maker who wants to use tasty fresh vegetables. I avoid store-bought tomatoes entirely. To add flavor to a green salad, I use one or two diced or sliced winter vegetables such as broccoli, cauliflower, Chinese cabbage, celery root, kohlrabi, chard or Jerusalem artichokes—in addition to the standbys of radishes, fresh carrots thinly sliced, or diced red onions. Red bell peppers, available in fall and early winter, are also a colorful and flavorful addition.

Vegie Pie

Preheat oven to 450°

Crust:

1 C white flour
½ C butter
dash of salt
1 T sugar

Sift dry ingredients together. Cut in butter with pastry blender. Press into 9-inch pie pan. Bake for 10 minutes. Reduce oven temperature to 350°.

Filling:

2 scallions, chopped fine
1 C sliced mushrooms
1 diced onion
1 C lightly steamed broccoli
1 C grated cheddar or swiss cheese
2 eggs
½ C milk
¼ C chopped parsley

Place the scallions, mushrooms, diced onion, and broccoli in the baked pie crust and sprinkle with the grated cheese. Mix together the eggs, milk, and parsley in a bowl and pour over the top. Season with salt and pepper to taste. Bake at 350° for 30-40 minutes until liquid solidifies.

Harriet's Cornbread

1½ C regular all purpose flour
3 t baking powder
dash of salt
1½ C yellow cornmeal
½ C corn, cut from the cob
½ C chopped green pepper
½ C chopped chili peppers, not too hot.
    If hot, use smaller quantity.
¼ C honey
⅛ C molasses
½ C salad oil
2 eggs, slightly beaten
1 C milk

Preheat oven to 400°.
Sift flour, baking powder and salt. Add cornmeal, corn, green peppers, and chili peppers. In a separate bowl, mix honey, molasses and salad oil. Add the eggs and milk. Add liquid ingredients to the dry ones, blending with swift strokes just until moistened. Pour into greased cast iron skillet and bake for 30 minutes. For a cornbread with a heavy crust, use bacon grease in the skillet and have it crackling hot when adding the cornbread mixture.

Chilled Spiced Carrots

Serves 4

6 medium carrots
1 C plain yogurt
3 T butter melted
1 t each chopped thyme, basil, and dill weed
1 t salt
½ t freshly ground pepper

Cut carrots lengthwise into quarters and boil until just tender. Mix all the remaining ingredients together and pour over carrots. Refrigerate for 1 hour before eating.

Stuffed Pierogi

(A Cream-Cheese Dough Stuffed with Mushrooms)

Dough:

1 C butter
8 oz. cream cheese
¼ cup heavy cream
3 cups flour
1 t salt
1 egg
1 t water

Cream the butter with the cheese and let it soften. Beat in the cream and then add 2¾ cups flour and the salt. Reserve the rest of the flour for use in rolling out. Chill the dough well.

When you are ready to make the *pierogi*, dust a large board or other flat surface with a little flour, dust the rolling pin with flour, and carefully roll out the dough to about ⅛-inch thickness. Test occasionally to be sure that the dough is not sticking to the board.

Cut the rolled dough into squares about 2½ inches in size. Into each square put a teaspoonful of the filling. Moisten the edges with a little egg beaten with the water, and bring the four corners up to the center. Seal the edges very carefully, as they have a tendency to come apart in baking if they are sloppy. When you are finished and ready to bake, brush the tops of the *pierogi* with a little more of the beaten egg.

Bake them in a preheated 375-degree oven for about 15 to 20 minutes, or until they are golden brown.

Filling:

5 oz. dried black mushrooms
1 large onion, finely chopped
3 T butter
2 slices black bread
2 t dill
2 hard-cooked eggs
salt and pepper
2 to 3 T sour cream (optional)

Soak the mushrooms in warm water until they are soft, about ½ hour or more. Drain off the water through cheesecloth and reserve it. Now wash the mushrooms very carefully, one by one if you must, to get rid of every bit of dirt. Put them through the food chopper on a coarse grind and sauté them with the chopped onion in the butter.

Soak the pieces of dry bread in the mushroom water and put them through the food chopper also before adding to the mushrooms and onion. Add the dill and season well with salt and pepper. Mash or sieve 2 hard-cooked eggs and stir them into the sautéing mixture. Taste and correct seasoning. At this point, if you would like a milder-flavored filling, add the sour cream. Otherwise, sauté about 10 minutes more, cool, and fill into the prepared dough.

Zucchini Fritata

Serves 3 or 4 as side dish, 2 as main course

1½ zucchini cut into ¼-inch slices
5 eggs, lightly beaten
1 T parsley chopped
2 T oil
¼ t each thyme, basil and oregano
3½ T parmesan
salt and pepper to taste

Heat oil in a medium sized omelet pan, add zucchini, and cook until lightly browned. Combine eggs, spices, cheese, and add salt and pepper to taste. Pour over zucchini and cook over medium heat until mixture almost sets, shaking pan occasionally. Sprinkle with cheese and place it briefly under the broiler until nicely browned.

Okra Fry

Serves 4

1 pound okra
1 C cornmeal
½ T salt
dash of cayenne
3 eggs
¼ C milk
Vegetable oil for frying

Slice the okra into ½ inch rounds. In a bowl, mix together the cornmeal, salt, and add a dash of cayenne. In another bowl, mix the eggs and milk together. Place ½ inch of oil in a deep frying pan and heat. Dip the okra in the egg and milk mixture, then into the cornmeal mixture, and drop into the hot oil. Fry until brown on one side, then fry on the other side. Drain on paper towels.

Phyllis' Green Beans

Serves 4

1 pound green beans, broken in half or cut, remove strings if present. Steam beans for 15 minutes. While beans are steaming, prepare a sauce in a heavy frying pan:

4 slices bacon, chopped
1½ onions chopped fine
1 clove garlic crushed or chopped fine
2 fresh tomatoes cut into quarters
dash of tabasco

Fry bacon slightly and then add garlic, onions, and tomatoes and cook until soft. Add tabasco. Add cooked green beans and briefly simmer together until heated through.

Green Eggs with Cheese

Serves 4

1 quart spinach, chard, or winter greens,
    washed well and drained
1 C chicken or vegetable broth
1 C grated cheddar cheese
4 eggs
2 C milk
salt and pepper to taste

Cook greens in the broth in a covered pot until barely tender, drain, then chop. Press cheese on the bottom and sides of a buttered 9-inch pie plate. Break eggs carefully over the cheese and keep yolks intact, 1 in each quadrant of the pie plate. Add salt and pepper. Dribble milk over the eggs, arrange greens around the eggs, bake in 350° oven until the eggs are set, about 10 minutes.

Fresh Corn

The rules for cooking fresh corn on the cob are simple. Buy it fresh, use it immediately or keep it in a cool place, and cook it briefly. Sugar in the corn turns quickly to starch, particularly if exposed to heat. This makes it important to buy corn that has just been cut and not exposed to much heat. If you are not going to serve the ears until later in the day, put them in a bag in a dark place or in the refrigerator. Don't be bothered that some ears may have worms. Those sections can be cut off when the corn is shucked. I doubt if there is any better method of preparation than inserting the ears in 3 inches of slightly salted boiling water and cooking each side of the ear for 2-3 minutes and serving them hot with plenty of salt, pepper, butter, and extra napkins on the table. I tend to be a purist and will cook several batches during a single meal as they are being eaten. This works better than letting the ears get cold on the table.

The kernels can be cut from any ears left over, inserted in a plastic bag, and placed in the freezer to be used when needed. While it is possible to freeze whole ears, this takes additional storage space and requires extra cooking time without any gain in flavor.

Baked corn has a somewhat different

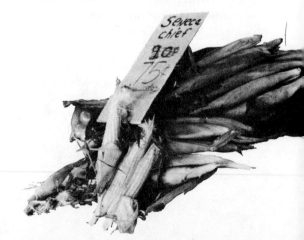

flavor, particularly if an open fire or pit has been used. For a beach picnic, dig a small pit in the sand. Dip individual unhusked ears in salt water, wrap in foil and bury, covering with a layer of sand or ashes so that the foil is no longer exposed. Build a fire above the sand layer and let cook for an hour. Tongs will be required for retrieving the baked corn. This will probably sound like heresy, but corn cooked in this way doesn't have to be completely fresh. The baking adds flavor of its own and 1- or 2-day old corn may be baked in its husk with satisfactory results. Baked corn tends to be more filling than boiled corn so you will probably need no more than 1-2 ears per person.

Boiling in sea water is a delicious idea.

Quick Vegetable Saute

Serves 4

2 T oil
¼ medium onion, diced
½ C green pepper, diced
1 clove garlic, crushed
4 C assorted summer squash (soft-skinned)
1½ C corn kernels
½ t each basil, marjoram, thyme
1 t salt
1 C tomato sauce
1½ C grated swiss cheese
parsley for garnish

Heat oil in a large skillet and saute onions, green pepper, and garlic. Add squash, corn, and spices. Stir over medium heat until squash is cooked. Add tomato sauce and simmer mixture over medium heat for about 5 minutes. Add cheese and stir until cheese is melted. Serve garnished with parsley.

Kohlrabi

Cut away tough exterior skin using a paring knife or cleaver. Kohlrabi may be diced and used uncooked in salads or cut into bite sized pieces which are boiled in slightly salted water for 20 minutes.

Drain and add nutmeg.

Chard Potatoes

Serves 4

Green portions of 6 leaves of fresh chard, chopped fine.*
*Kale or spinach leaves may be substituted.

2 lbs. of white medium sized potatoes, peeled and chopped into quarters
2 T milk
2 T butter
5 C water
½ t salt

Add chopped chard to 2 cups of lightly salted water, bring to a boil, and cook for 10 minutes.

In a separate container, cover the quartered potatoes with water, salt lightly, and cook until soft.

Drain chard and potatoes, and combine them in a single container. Add the milk and butter, crush all ingredients and stir. Season to taste and serve hot.

Jerusalem Artichokes

Serves 4

The Jerusalem artichoke is a tuber of the sunflower family and bears no relationship to the globe artichoke. Jerusalem is a corruption of the Italian word for sunflower. This tuber has a distinct nutty taste and can be used fresh-sliced in a green salad, or cooked in place of potatoes. Wrapped in foil, with a bit of butter and salt, it can be placed under the embers of the fire and baked for 15 minutes.

Home-Fried Jerusalem Artichokes

Serves 4

8 bulbs cut into half-inch sections
2 buds of fresh shallots, finely chopped
    or 2 T of dried shallots
¼ T butter
3 T vegetable oil

Saute the shallots in the butter for 5 minutes. Put the oil in a heavy frying pan over medium heat, add the artichoke slices and the shallots and cook approximately 10 minutes until the slices are reasonably soft.

Remove artichokes from pan and let stand on absorbent paper to soak up excess oil. Keep in warm oven until ready to use. This will crispen the slices. Salt to taste.

Vegetarian Sukiyaki

Serves 3-4

1½ C chicken or vegetable stock
2 T soy sauce
2 T worcestershire sauce
2 T honey
1 C grated carrots
1 C chopped summer squash
½ C sliced mushrooms
1 C chopped cabbage or bok choy
1 C mashed tofu

Combine stock, sauces, and honey in a large skillet, bring to a boil and add carrots, squash, and mushrooms. Simmer at medium heat until tender. Reduce heat and add cabbage and tofu. Cook about 3 minutes still at medium heat. Serve by itself or with rice in large soup bowls.

Davis, CALIFORNIA

"Fresher by Miles," a 16 mm color movie developed by the New Jersey Department of Agriculture dealing with farmer-to-consumer sales, is available on loan or purchase from the Division of Marketing, Department of Agriculture, P.O. Box 188, Trenton, New Jersey 98625. 13 minutes long.

"Planning Farmers' Markets" and "Selling at Farmers' Markets," two slide-tape sets prepared by Jim Bell and Marilyn Grantham, available from the Department of Agricultural Economics, Virginia Polytechnic Institute and State University, Blacksburg, Va. 24061.

Narrative slide series of Massachusetts Farm Markets. Regarding availability contact R. Alden Miller, Regional Vegetable Specialist, 36 Harvard Street, Worcester, Mass. 01608.

Direct Marketing Newsletter, available from the Department of Agricultural Economics, Warren Hall, Cornell University, Ithaca, NY 14853.

Organic Gardening and Farming is a monthly magazine that has frequent articles about farmer-to-consumer sales.

California Agricultural Direct Marketing Guide, available without charge from California State Department of Consumer Affairs, Sacramento, CA 95814.

Proceedings of the 1978 Illinois Community-Farm Market Conference and **Proceedings of the 1979 Illinois Community-Farm Market Conference,** two volumes crammed full of information about establishing, running, and publicizing farmers' markets, are obtainable for $2 each from the Department of Horticulture, University of Illinois, 124 Mumford Hall, Urbana, IL 61801.

"Organizing Food Fairs." Videotape available from Agricultural Marketing Project, 2602 Westwood Drive, Nashville, TENN 37204.

"How to Create a Farmers' Market." Pamphlet distributed without charge by the Pennsylvania Department of Agriculture, 2301 North Cameron Street, Harrisburg, PA 17120.

Barry Benepe, **Greenmarket: The Rebirth of Farmers' Markets in New York City.** A pamphlet describing the New York City Greenmarket Program is obtainable for $2 from the Council on the Environment of New York City, 51 Chambers Street, New York City 10007.

Farmers' Market Organizers Handbook. Mimeographed booklet obtainable for $1 from the Hunger Action Center, Room 206, 1063 Capitol Way, Olympia, WA 98501.

"Organization and Operation of Louisiana Farmers' Markets," "Sellers of Produce at Louisiana Farmers' Markets," and "Customer Evaluation of Farmers' Markets in Louisiana." Three reports distributed without cost by the Department of Agricultural Economics and Agribusiness, Louisiana State University, Baton Rouge, LA 70803.

Kathy Cecil, **Food From Farmers** (1978). $3.00. Obtainable from Earthwork, 3410-19th Street, San Francisco, CA 94110. A guide to direct marketing operations in Northern California, also contains home processing information and recipes.

Organizing a Farmers' Market. Mimeographed booklet distributed without cost by the Direct Marketing Program, 1220 N Street, Sacramento, CA 95814.

Foreword   **Two Japanese writers:** Hiroshi Isogai and Shunjiro Matsushima, *Market Places of the World.* Palo Alto, California: Kodansha International Limited, 1972.

p. 14   **One economist estimated:** Morris L. Sweet, History of municipal markets. Journal of Housing, 1961, *18,* 237-247.

p. 24   **A regional warehouse:** Padraic Burke, Reviving the urban market, "Don't fix it up too much." *Nation's Cities,* February 1978, 9-12.

p. 26   **The district commission in Washington, D.C.:** Burke, *op. cit.*

p. 27   **The agricultural policies of the Consumers Federation of America:** Kathleen F. O'Reilly, Testimony before the Committee on Agriculture, U.S. House of Representatives, March 3, 1977.

p. 35   **Today that figure is less than 30¢:** U.S.D.A., 1975 Handbook of Agricultural Charts. Washington: Government Printing Office, 1975.

p. 35   **Taking into account the increased expenses:** Curtis J. Moulton, "King County Agricultural Marketing Study." Report prepared for the King County Office of Agriculture, October 1977.

p. 36   **Geils found the advantages so great:** Ervin Geils, Farmers Markets—A producer's Viewpoint. Proceedings of the 1978 Illinois Community Farm Market Conference. Villa Park, Illinois: Cooperative Extension Service, March 22, 1978.

p. 36   **Farmers selling at the Detroit Eastern Farmers Market:** Pamela Marshall De Weese, The Detroit Eastern Farmers Market: Its social structure and functions. Detroit: Center for Urban Studies, Ethnic Studies Division, Wayne State University, November 1975.

p. 36   **A survey of small farmers:** Moulton, *op. cit.*

p. 44   **Supermarket prices in Hartford, Conn.:** Sally Taylor, Food, home grown—how long? The Hartford Courant, April 26, 1979.

p. 44   **Studies in four Southeastern states:** VPI, Planning a Farmers Market. Publication 776, Extension Division, Virginia Polytechnic Institute and State University, June 1978.

p. 44   **A study of food fairs . . . in Tennessee and Alabama:** AMP, "Cost Benefit Analysis for Food Fairs in Tennessee and Alabama." Report distributed by Agricultural Marketing Project, Vanderbilt Medical Center, Station 17, Nashville, Tenn., 1977.

p. 44   **A food price survey in Seattle:** Pike Place Merchants Association, "Food Price Survey: Locally Grown Produce." Mimeographed Report, August 21, 1978.

p. 46   **Research has shown that green-picked tomatoes:** Adel A. Kader, M. Allen Stevens, Marjorie Albright-Holton, Leonard L. Morris, and Margaret Algazi, Effect of fruit ripeness when picked on flavor and composition in fresh market tomatoes. Journal of the *American Society for Horticultural Science,* 1977, *102,* 724-733.

p. 46   **Systematic laboratory studies:** R. Sommer, H. Knight, and B.A. Sommer. Comparison of farmers market and supermarket produce: tomatoes and bell peppers. *Journal of Food Science,* 1979, *44,* 1474-1477.

p. 52   **The Dutin Farmers Market:** John L. Hess, Return of a farmers market. *Organic Gardening and Farming,* 1974, *21,* 64-7.

p. 53   **Durham, North Carolina, Revitalization Foundation:** Joanne B. Winslow, Downtown. *American City and County,* October 1975.

p. 53   **The Alpena, Michigan, open air market:** Mary Zehner, How to organize and operate a successfully municipally sponsored retail farmers market. Talk given at the 1979 Direct Marketing Workshop, Chicago, Illinois, April 17-19, 1979.

p. 54   **The Kitchener, Ontario, Market:** Anne Kloppenborg, To market, to market. *Urban Reader,* 1977, *5,* 2-8.

p. 72   **In 1972, two Japanese writers:** Isogai and Matsushima, *op. cit.*

p. 72   **The private sales barn in Moorefield, West Virginia:** Pyle, *op. cit.*

p. 72   **The Paterson Market:** Joan Cook, Farmers market in Paterson is thriving. *New York Times,* September 15, 1975, p. 43.

p. 72   **The Trenton Farmers Market:** James W. Fernandez, The world, old and new in the Trenton Farmers Market. New York Times, June 12, 1976, section 1, p. 23.

p. 73   **The Tomales Bay, California, Vegetable Swap:** Carole Turko, Tips from other farmers markets. *Organic Gardening and Farming,* 1976, *23,* 111-113.

PRODUCTION

Cover and text design by Mary Schlesinger.
Production assistance, Terri Wright.
Typesetting by McAdams Type.

Camera work by Santa Barbara Photoengraving.
Cover printed by Haagen Printing, Santa Barbara.
Text printed and bound by R.R. Donnelley & Sons.

Photos in text taken by:

Frank Becker, pp. 21, 41, 43, 75, 77, 96
Hank Bennet, pp. 25, 46, 50, 69, 70, 86
Alan Elms, pp. 42, 47 (Greenmarket)
Jason Tyburczy, pp. 11, 15
Margaret Wing, pp. 3, 37, 73, 81
Peter Mohrmann, back cover

All others by the author.

Canvas Craft: The Homesewer's Guide to Creating Useful and Delightful Objects from a Noble Cloth; *Susan Dworski.*

The Toilet Papers: Designs to Recycle Human Waste and Water: Dry Toilets, Greywater Systems, & Urban Sewage; *Sim Van der Ryn.*

Rescued Buildings: The Art of Living in Former Schoolhouses, Skating Rinks, Fire Stations, Churches, Barns, Summer Camps and Cabooses; *Roland Jacopetti and Ben Vanmeter.*

Sweat: The Illustrated History and Description of the Finnish Sauna, Russian Bania, Islamic Hammam, Japanese Mushi-buro, Mexican Temescal and American Indian & Eskimo Sweat Lodge; *Mikkel Aaland.*

Hot Springs and Pools of the Southwest; *Jayson Loam.*

Hot Springs and Pools of the Northwest; *Jayson Loam.*

Oasis: The Complete Guide to Bottled Water Throughout the World; *Arthur von Wiesenberger.*

Mud Space & Spirit: Handmade Adobes; *Virginia Gray and Alan Macrae.*

Foraging Along The California Coast: The Complete Illustrated Handbook; *Peter Howorth.*

Condor Journal: The History, Mythology and Reality of the California Condor; *Dick Smith.*